Malcolm Groves, A
and **John West-Burnham**

Leadership
for Tomorrow

Beyond the School
Improvement Horizon

Crown House Publishing Limited
www.crownhouse.co.uk

First published by

Crown House Publishing
Crown Buildings,
Bancyfelin,
Carmarthen,
Wales, SA33 5ND, UK
www.crownhouse.co.uk

and

Crown House Publishing Company LLC
PO Box 2223, Williston, VT 05495, USA
www.crownhousepublishing.com

Quotes from Ofsted and Department for Education documents used in this publication have been approved under an Open Government Licence. Please see: http://www.nationalarchives.gov.uk/doc/open-government-licence/version/3/.

Select quotes and case studies referred to in this publication are taken from research conducted by the authors over a number of years. These studies have been variously published in:

Groves, M. (2014). An Investigation into the Inter-Connectedness of Trust, Community Engagement, School Leadership and Educational Outcomes in English Secondary Schools. PhD thesis, Centre for Education Studies, University of Warwick.

Groves, M. (2016). *Bedford Schools Well-being Strategy: An Evaluation*. Bedford: Peter Pan Teaching School Alliance.

The Beauchamp Papers (2013–2015), a free, online series of think pieces, research, and practical case studies of change, published by Schools of Tomorrow. See: http://www.schoolsoftomorrow.org/styled-3/.

Material from the report and papers are used with permission of the respective organisational chairs and with thanks to the research participants.

Crown House Publishing has no responsibility for the persistence or accuracy of URLs for external or third-party websites referred to in this publication, and does not guarantee that any content on such websites is, or will remain, accurate or appropriate.

British Library Cataloguing-in-Publication Data

A catalogue entry for this book is available from the British Library.

Print ISBN: 978-178583237-6
Mobi ISBN: 978-178583296-3
ePub ISBN: 978-178583297-0
ePDF ISBN: 978-178583298-7

LCCN 2017957036

Printed and bound in the UK by TJ International, Padstow, Cornwall

For all who are striving today to be leaders for tomorrow.

Contents

List of figures

Preface

This book is about and for school leaders who understand that they must live and lead in overlapping, often conflicting, and frequently ambiguous and uncertain worlds – which we broadly choose to characterise as the worlds of today and tomorrow – and who want to be better able to do that. It is also for anyone who in any way holds school leaders to account, as well as those who may look to lead the schools of tomorrow.

It is the result of nearly a decade of thinking, research, and observation of leadership practice which we have undertaken in a range of settings. We have written up some of this experience previously in a series of pamphlets called The Beauchamp Papers, developed for those school leaders who were involved in establishing a new research and development network of schools in England under the name Schools of Tomorrow. We have drawn on their work in writing this book. Whilst the book is focused on changes within the English educational system, we hope that the lessons derived from this will be of interest to leaders in other school systems.

The five leaders featured in this book have been the subject of intensive study over a number of years. Each has been the subject of in-depth, semi-structured interviews with at least one of the authors on more than one occasion over a three-year period (2013–2016), as have members of their leadership teams. School documentation has also been examined.[1] In some cases, the views of other stakeholders, including students, have been sought. In addition, the work of two of the leaders has been the subject of more intensive study and research over a longer period as part of a doctoral thesis completed by Malcolm Groves at the University of Warwick.

What we have attempted to do here, however, is to draw all this thinking and practical experience together into a coherent whole. We have sought to project the meaning and implications forward into a new phase of school improvement, in the hope that this will assist others, both in the UK and internationally, engaged in leading or wishing to lead their schools beyond today's limited school improvement horizon.

---

1   All school information is correct as of December 2016.

Part One:
The Case for Change

Introduction:
Three Horizons

In the first two decades of the twenty-first century, leaders of schools in England have been caught up in an almost bewildering vortex of swirling cross-currents and riptides as national policy has veered first in one direction, then in another. The forces which have given rise to this instability are, though, not unique to one country. They are better understood as part of a much wider phenomenon, even though some responses may be peculiar to English politics. In general, we cannot seem to agree on the purpose and rationale of our education provision.

Education is a significant example of an 'essentially contested concept'. These, according to Gallie's definition of the phrase, 'inevitably involve endless disputes about their proper uses on the part of their users' (1955: 169). For Guy Claxton and Bill Lucas (2015), this dispute in education is characterised as being between three groups. The romantics (roms) are so defined because of their belief in the innate goodness of children, who, by virtue of this innate quality, have no need for didactic teaching or adult authority. The traditionalists (trads), on the other hand, are so called due to their view of teachers as respected sources of culturally important tried and tested factual knowledge which they pass on to children and then test receipt of through formal examination. A third group, the moderates (mods), Claxton and Lucas suggest, reject this simplistic duality, understand complexity, do not believe in quick fixes or appeals to nostalgia, and so think, tinker, and explore so as to better understand the nature of learning. This book is essentially written from a mod viewpoint.

Educational discourse abounds with polarising spectrums – traditional or progressive, academic or vocational, skills or knowledge, and many more. This often contested theoretical space is also inevitably the territory in which school leaders exist and live, and through which they must move, having the direct responsibility to chart a course in the best interests of the young people in their care.

We believe, though, that there is now something more fundamental happening to education than suggested by these long-held, strongly argued debates. We think the present upheavals are in fact symptoms of a more terminal problem with our present concept of schooling, designed as it was to serve the purposes of different times and often reflecting the mindset of an analogue, pre-digital age.

A good analogy to help understand this can be borrowed from the energy industry. According to Curry and Hodgson (2008), the challenge of achieving a sustainable energy supply can be conceptualised using the lens of three different horizons (see Figure 1). The first horizon represents the way we generate and use energy at present. It is inefficient, damaging to the environment, short-term, and ultimately unsustainable. A third horizon represents the outlook of those who have seen these limitations and are trying to create alternative, viable, sustainable solutions to meet future energy needs. These might include, for example, solar and wind power, hydrogen cells, biofuels, and changing consumption patterns. Such solutions are currently still experimental, are not yet proven, may be contradictory, and none are yet to scale or fully tested. However, at some point in the future, a new way forward will emerge from this experimental cauldron to supersede the unsustainable status quo.

Between these points lies another conceptual horizon, termed the second horizon, falling as it does between now and the future. This is the space in which leaders try to make sense of and navigate between the failing, unsustainable present and the as yet uncertain future, in order to create a meaningful future for their organisation, and, in the case of schools, for those in their care. For one big difference between running a school and a running an energy business lies in the fact that what school leaders do and how they do it directly shapes individual lives now, as well as impacting on the futures those individuals are able to create for themselves.

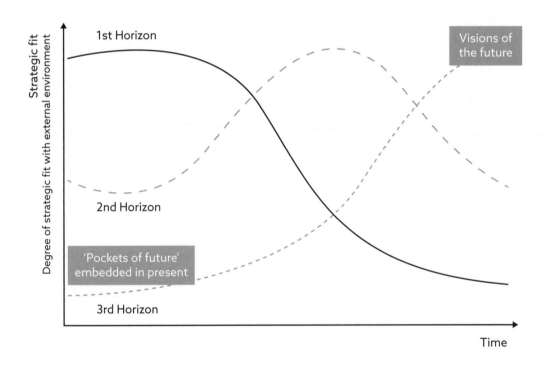

Figure 1: The three-horizon model (Curry and Hodgson, 2008: 2)
Reproduced with kind permission of the *Journal of Futures Studies*

The parallel of the original model for education leadership is uncanny. As Claxton and Lucas (2015) show, there is a strong body of opinion which recognises that our present concept of schooling in terms of its purpose and our understanding of quality are reaching the end of their useful life. There is, as well, a range of alternative thinking going on, frequently small scale, unproven, and often on the basis of individual enthusiasms. Think perhaps of studio schools, some free schools, or project-based learning (PBL) amongst many other initiatives.

But for a school leader, there is never going to be a completely clean slate from which to start, a day in the future when everything can begin afresh and be wholly reconstituted from the ground up. There are always real children to be educated today, who have a single best shot at their own future. There will always, legitimately, be government expectations to meet, although these may be more or less helpful. So leaders of change have no choice but to build their future plane in the sky as they fly it, rather than work on it in its hangar.

For these leaders, the role of leadership is therefore not confined simply to responding to the short-term demands of today, driven by government accountability alone. Leadership must mesh this with a clear vision of what is needed for tomorrow and a determination to find practical and effective ways to start moving towards that – within the constraints of today.

This means living and leading in two worlds at one and the same time, and it means living with the tension and ambiguity which that necessarily involves. Of course, the balance between the two worlds may shift according to context, circumstance, and capacity. But leadership for tomorrow is actually an integral part of leading effectively today. Furthermore, leading for today will ultimately not succeed if it fails to lead for tomorrow as well.

The central task of this book is to show how some leaders are already setting about using this tension creatively to start to fashion better futures for the children and young people in their care. In doing this, we hope to encourage others in positions of leadership and influence to go further in building their own and their schools' capacity to live and grow successfully towards the second horizon, bringing together and into a new relationship the worlds of today and tomorrow.

The origins of *Leadership for Tomorrow*

This book's origins lie in many places. It began, most obviously, through the work of a small group of school leaders in England, who met together one day in November 2011 at Beauchamp College, Leicester, to ponder whether there was any contribution they could make to collectively shape a better future for their schools. As a result, they formed a small research and development group, which they came to call Schools of Tomorrow,[1] to support schools and school leaders who wanted to explore second horizon thinking and practice. Their experience and practice has directly informed the development of this book.

---

1   See www.schoolsoftomorrow.org.

Another, more removed, origin lies in the intriguing story of the American township of Roseto (Gladwell, 2009). This close-knit Italian-American community in Pennsylvania was the focus of health studies for nearly 50 years, after it was noticed that heart disease was much less prevalent there than in the nearby similar community of Bangor. Wolf and Bruhn (1993), reviewing studies made of Roseto between 1935 and 1984, conclude that mutual respect and cooperation contribute to the health and welfare of a community's inhabitants, and that self-indulgence and lack of concern for others have the opposite effect. They found that belonging to a tight-knit community was a better predictor of healthy hearts than low levels of serum cholesterol or abstaining from tobacco use.

More recently, Holt-Lunstad et al. (2010), looking more broadly at data from 148 studies totalling 308,849 participants, echoed the link between relationships and health, concluding that the influence of limited social relationships on mortality risk is comparable with other well-established risk factors, and exceeds many.

There is one further significant feature to pick out from the story of Roseto. The leadership of the parish priest, Rev. Pasquale de Nisco, was crucial in forging and sustaining the social networks and trust which underpinned Rosetan life in its early days (Bruhn and Wolf, 1979: 13–20). Arriving in Roseto in June 1897, he found a disorganised, disparate group of Italian immigrants clinging to their land, knowing little English and almost nothing of their new country. There was no coordination of effort and no grasp of citizenship. De Nisco set up spiritual societies and organised festivals. He also initiated projects to improve the diet of the population though planting gardens and vineyards and raising livestock. Gradually Rosetans developed a sense of civic pride and began to build civic amenities. Additionally, increased enterprise meant more employment opportunities. The town had started to come alive through the priest's leadership, and that social interaction, Wolf and Bruhn demonstrated, had profound implications for physical health.

The story of Roseto is illuminating as a specific case study of the significance of social capital and its impact on one aspect of human development over time, as are the unique circumstances which allowed that to happen. Of course, Roseto was not perfect, and some would now regard it as an unduly restrictive community, not one we might choose to live in ourselves. However, it reminds us that so-called outliers can reveal important insights for 'normal' practice. It also says something important about the significance of leadership in building and shaping social capital, for better or indeed for worse.

Building social capital is something we believe to be critically important for leadership, Although a complex and to some extent contested concept, most definitions of the term would include the following elements:

- A high degree of consensus around norms and values that actively inform day-to-day interactions.
- A shared language with a specialist vocabulary that enables open and lateral communication.
- A strong sense of shared identity and interdependence working through rich networks and a sense of mutual responsibility.

- Active involvement and participation in the working of the community – standing for office, voting, and accepting civic responsibility.
- A commitment to openness and sharing ideas and wisdom.
- A shared sense of purpose and optimism for the future.

Field (2008: 1) helpfully sums up the complicated concept of social capital quite succinctly:

> The theory of social capital is, at heart, most straightforward. Its central thesis can be summed up in two words: relationships matter. By making connections with one another, and keeping them going over time, people are able to work together to achieve things that they either could not achieve by themselves, or could only achieve with great difficulty. People connect through a series of networks, and they tend to share common values with other members of these networks.

But could changes in social capital influence educational outcomes in ways similar to their reported impact on health? If so, what forms could this influence take, how does it arise, and what might that impact be? Particularly, what does it mean for individual leaders who want to secure the best outcomes for all their pupils, and for the nature of their leadership? These questions are particularly pertinent for leaders who grasp the significance of the second horizon, at a time when new concerns have been raised about how well we are educating our young people in the context of a globalised economy. A context which is increasingly competitive at both a national and personal level, but also reveals major issues of fairness and sustainability. The influence and significance of social capital is a key theme to which we will frequently return.

Significance in the present context of English schools

One of the first actions of the coalition government which took office in the UK in May 2010 was to change the name of the Department of Children, Schools and Families (DCSF) to the Department for Education (DfE). This gesture was intended to symbolise a renewed focus on the core business of teaching and learning. The subsequent White Paper (Department for Education, 2010: 8) stressed that: 'Our school system performs well below its potential and can improve significantly. Many other countries in the world are improving their schools faster than we are.'

As part of the government's refocusing of expectations on schools, a number of inherited policies which suggested that schools had some wider role in support of families and communities were changed or abandoned. The distinct funding for the specialist schools programme, which required such schools to share skills and resources across their communities, was no longer ring fenced, expectations around extended school provision were removed, and focus on the Every Child Matters agenda was much reduced.

A raft of other policy changes have included a focus on a narrower range of educational outcomes in terms of definition of attainment, with a stress on academic rigour in a reduced range of curriculum subjects. There is also a greater reliance on test-based assessment, with an associated return to norm-referencing, by which only a given percentage of students succeed, rather than criterion-referencing, offering success for all who meet a given standard, as in a driving test or passing a music grade.

At the same time, significant changes were made to the academies programme inherited from the previous government, with the focus shifting from academy status as a mechanism for improving those underperforming schools operating in very challenging environments to one which outstanding schools were encouraged to adopt. By the time of the 2016 White Paper, *Education Excellence Everywhere* (Department for Education, 2016), there was an unequivocal wish by government for all schools to become academies within the framework of a multi-academy trust (MAT), even though they subsequently rowed back a little from the notion of explicit compulsion.

This direction of travel is perceived as part of a move towards a self-improving school system. This notion of system leadership, and the related concept of self-improving schools, is strongly articulated by Hargreaves (2011: 8), who stresses the connections between schools in supporting each other to reach school-focused ends:

> A maturity model of a self-improving school system is a statement of the organisational and professional practices of two or more schools in partnership by which they progressively achieve shared goals, both local and systemic.

System leadership is also strongly focused within that maturity model around the role of the head teacher (Boylan, 2016). Such thinking has been a key element in government policy in England since 2010. According to the White Paper of that year, *The Importance of Teaching*:

> The primary responsibility for improvement rests with schools ... Our aim should be to create a school system which is more effectively self-improving. (Department for Education, 2010: 13)

Many subsequent government reforms were directed towards such ends. For example, the National College for Teaching and Leadership (NCTL) was established in 2013 'to enable and support the development of a self-improving, school-led system', although, as Greany (2015: 7) observes, the addition of 'school-led' alongside 'self-improving' is notable, since the two concepts are not necessarily the same. The principle was also endorsed by leading UK professional associations, such as the Association of School and College Leaders (ASCL) in their *Blueprint for a Self-Improving System* (Cruddas, 2015).

This book, however, will argue that the notion of system leadership thus described offers only a partial picture of what is needed if its place and purpose is to effect long-term improvement. We suggest that there is an additional need to understand system leadership more broadly: acting between the school, the learners, their families, and communities, causing each to interact differently with the others so as to promote both broader and improved learning outcomes. This inevitably highlights the need for greater understanding of complexity, a key theme of this book, and an associated deeper understanding of change and how it happens.

For many years, school improvement has been focused on the quality of teaching and learning in classrooms. The necessity of that focus will not in any way be challenged here. Rather, our argument is that, whilst necessary and important, on its own it is not sufficient either to develop fully that broader set of skills and attitudes which will equip young people to flourish in a rapidly changing world or to bring about sustainable long-term change in schools, especially within local cultures of educational indifference and low aspiration.

Behind many of these often government-imposed changes to classroom practice – in relation to pedagogy, curriculum, and assessment – lies a very strong policy concern to 'narrow the gap' in terms of the impact of social disadvantage on educational attainment. We believe this is sincere and right in intent, but will argue that the resulting strategy has only partly diagnosed the treatment needed, addresses symptoms not causes, and will, therefore, ultimately not be able to succeed.

Counter-indicators

The suggestion that schools may have some wider role than teaching and learning, important as this is, and that there could be benefit in schools focusing more explicitly on their role in developing social capital, might therefore be seen as going against the grain of much current national education policy. But this idea is certainly not new. A range of counter-indicators over the last two decades have pointed to the possibility of a closer connection between high social capital and educational attainment than recent government policy initiatives would suggest. We briefly highlight just three here.

Firstly, research published by the Audit Commission (2006) in England concluded that schools, particularly in the most deprived areas, need to be proactive in building social capital in order to overcome socio-economic disadvantage and bring about school improvement. Their report argued that the issues of school improvement and renewal are inseparable from neighbourhood improvement and renewal, particularly in the most disadvantaged areas. It concluded that, whilst schools are profoundly affected by their neighbourhoods, they equally have a key role in promoting cohesion and building social capital. We shall examine the implications of this further in Chapter 1.

Secondly, a series of reports by UNICEF has indicated a possible connection between children and young people's well-being and their learning. The study attempted to measure the well-being of children and young people in 21 countries using the following criteria: material well-being, health and safety, educational well-being, family and peer relationships, behaviours and risks, and subjective well-being.

Using the 2007 report as an example, the UK was in the bottom third in all aspects of well-being except health and safety, where it was ranked 12th (UNICEF, 2007). It was the only country, apart from the United States, to be ranked in the bottom third in all but one aspects. Of those countries in the top third for educational well-being, four out of seven were also in the top third for at least four other aspects. We shall explore the significance of this further, and look at more recent data, when we turn specifically to well-being in Chapter 5.

Finally, there is a small though growing critique of the assessment measurements by which school effectiveness has come to be judged, whilst the data these generate form the underpinning of many government policies. Gorard (2009: 756) argues, from a viewpoint of deep statistical understanding, that when it comes to the statistical models used to measure school effectiveness:

> the field as a whole simply ignores these quite elementary logical problems, while devising more and more complex models comprehended by fewer and fewer people.

He continues by relating the statistical problem to a critique of current models for school effectiveness, that it:

> encourages, unwittingly, an emphasis on assessment and test scores – and teaching to the test – because over time we tend to get the system we measure for and so privilege. (Gorard, 2009: 759)

This leads him to his key conclusion:

> One clear finding that is now largely unremarked by academics and unused by policy-makers is that pupil prior attainment and background explain the vast majority of variation in school outcomes. (Gorard, 2009: 761)

We will return to the significance of this crucial and fundamental point in Chapter 1.

In the context of recent policy change, these criticisms and counter-indicators suggest it might be a particularly apt time to try to understand more fully the ways in which social capital and educational outcomes may be connected, the influence one may have on the other, and the possible implications for school leaders who understand the imperative to look towards tomorrow.

To help us do that, we have divided the book into three parts. These parts deliberately interweave theory and practice, though we are mindful of the wisdom attributed to Yogi Berra: 'In theory, there is no difference between theory and practice. In practice, there is.'

Much of the theory is concentrated in Part One. Its main concern is to set out and justify the principles and values from which we are working, as well as signpost the evidence which highlights the limitations of first horizon thinking and justifies why we think it is destined to fail. Part Two is more concerned with practice. It uses case studies based on interviews with five leaders to look at how those principles and values are being developed in real schools today. Part Three then attempts to bring theory and practice together to construct approaches to school improvement moving forward, which are at one and the same time values based and evidence informed.

Although there are significant lines of argument that run through the book in what we hope is a coherent and cumulative way, you may also want to chart a less linear route through it for yourself and dip into the three parts in a different order. For our part, we will try to assist you by providing regular signposts backwards and forwards to connecting parts of the book. This is intended to be a reflective book. It is not speculative, but rather grounded in solid evidence. We have referenced the book fully so that you can pursue any aspect in further depth or check our interpretation, if you wish. Throughout the book, we will also seek to create opportunities for your reflection as a reader, and we encourage you to pause at suitable stages to draw on and compare your own ideas and experience.

David Hargreaves (2001: 493) has criticised traditional models and understanding of leadership and school improvement, arguing that they largely ignore what he termed 'the impact of the moral excellences and the underpinning social capital on the optimisation of intellectual capital'. He cited, by way of example, the common description of a head teacher's leadership as 'purposeful', finding it 'worryingly bland':

> It is not *any* purpose that matters: the nature and perceived legitimacy of the goals involved is critical to the purposefulness that a leader demonstrates. Moreover, leadership is concerned with the means of realising the goals, both their efficiency and morality, not only the goals themselves. (Hargreaves, 2001: 491)

The five school and MAT leaders that we shall meet in Part Two, who inhabit the second horizon – bridging today and tomorrow – understand the impact of both moral purpose and social capital. They have thought deeply about the nature of their goals. As a result, they are reaching for a deeper and broader understanding of the purpose of schooling, and therefore of what constitutes true quality.

Before we look in some depth at their experience, we want to do three particular things in Part One to set out a justification and context for their work, and to help us understand the bigger picture in which they are operating.

Firstly, we want to pursue further Hargreaves' question of moral purpose by setting out the values and principles which underpin our understanding of leadership for tomorrow, along with the reasoning and evidence which gives rise to these. We will also start to introduce what we see as some of the implications for leadership flowing from these values and principles, which we will then glimpse in the practice of these leaders.

Secondly, we will look a bit further into the present direction of travel of the English school system, currently engaged in perhaps the biggest systemic upheaval in a hundred years, to try to enhance the understanding both of those who have to lead schools successfully through this confused and in many ways contradictory landscape, as well as those from other countries who may want to draw important wider lessons from this experience and will in any case be facing similar tensions from competing horizons.

Finally, by identifying some trends that have significant implications for learning, we will try to form a better understanding of the world of tomorrow for which we are preparing young people, whilst accepting that predictions are always notoriously difficult to make – especially when they are about the future!

Questions for reflection and discussion

- To what extent do you think educational outcomes can be influenced by changes in social capital, bearing in mind their reported impact on health outcomes? What leads you to take that view?
- What is your understanding of the purpose of schooling? How well is this reflected in practice in your school or in schools that you know well?
- What priority do you currently give in your leadership to building social capital within and outside your school?
- How far do you see yourself as someone who has the capacity and desire to make a difference to your school and its communities?

Chapter 1
Values and Principles:
Four Propositions

In seeking to discuss the characteristics of an outstanding school of tomorrow we feel we must exercise a necessary caution. At its worst this could become a dogmatic extension of current thinking or, at best, an aspirational scenario so fraught with contradictory variables that it appears naive or utopian. However, if the dictum 'the future does not exist, we create it' is taken as a starting premise, then perhaps there might be greater grounds for optimism. We create our personal and collective futures by making choices that move us closer to our preferred future state.

Education policy-making always seems to be a balancing act between evidence and dogma, with successive governments being located at various points on the spectrum. Of course, one person's dogma is another person's evidence. Objectivity is elusive in almost every aspect of educational decision-making; perhaps one can only hope to be less subjective. Any debate about the nature of the outstanding school of tomorrow is also beset by the endemic political short-termism of educational policy-making, with the inevitable disjointed incrementalism that results. For example, there is abundant and compelling evidence that investment in the early years is one of the most powerful ways of improving educational outcomes of all types. Yet pre-school provision is, along with 16–19 provision, a significant casualty of financial cutbacks; witness the closure of children's centres and the Every Child Matters programme.

The ethical basis for leading a school of tomorrow

The very concept of the outstanding school of tomorrow is bound to be problematic and contentious in the absence of any sort of national consensus as to what constitutes an effective education, let alone an outstanding one. This chapter is therefore based on the consideration of four key points:

1   The ethical foundations that should inform any discussion about education in the future.

2   The significance of the social factors influencing educational success.

3   The development of strategies to secure outstanding teaching and learning for all.

4   The leadership that is necessary to help successfully move today towards tomorrow.

We will examine each of these points in turn, beginning with a proposition, then setting out the evidence and argument in support, and we will encourage you to think and reflect about possible implications for your leadership and for your school. In Part Two of the book, you will have a chance to look closely at how five school leaders have developed their role and their school in practice as a result of such thinking.

Proposition 1

The outstanding school of tomorrow is one in which every child is entitled to a holistic educational experience which is rooted in personal well-being, is delivered on the basis of equity, and is responsive to the personal needs of every learner.

The school is thus defined in essentially moral terms with an explicit focus on the overarching entitlement of every child to well-being, which includes – but is more than – exceptional levels of personal achievement. That means the school develops a culture, and secures systems and strategies, to embed equity and inclusion, starting from the premise of the centrality of the needs of the vulnerable.

Article 29 of the United Nations Convention on the Rights of the Child (UNICEF, 1989) offers a very clear view of the moral basis of education and the entitlement of every child, which should include:

e. The development of the child's personality, talents, and mental and physical abilities to their fullest potential.

f. The development of respect for human rights and fundamental freedoms, and for the principles enshrined in the Charter of the United Nations.

g. The development of respect for the child's parents, his or her own cultural identity, language and values, for the national values of the country in which the child is living, the country from which he or she may originate, and for civilisations different from his or her own.

h. The preparation of the child for responsible life in a free society, in the spirit of understanding, peace, tolerance, equality of sexes, and friendship among all peoples, ethnic, national and religious groups and persons of indigenous origin.

i. The development of respect for the natural environment.

This view seems to point to an implicit fundamental ethical framework based on supporting the well-being of each child, and the importance of a holistic model of education. Michael Fullan (2007: 11) argues that there is a close reinforcing link between well-being and educational achievement:

Well-being serves as a double duty. It directly supports literacy and numeracy; that is, emotional health is strongly associated with cognitive achievement. It also is indirectly but powerfully part of the educational and societal goal of dealing with the emotional and social consequences of failing and being of low status. In this sense, political leaders must have an explicit agenda of well-being, of which education is one powerful component.

Accepting the importance of a well-being agenda, what follows from this perspective is the pivotal importance of equity as a guiding concept. The challenge here is that most educational systems have achieved a high degree of equality – everybody has the right to go to school – but many systems have a long way to go with regard to equity, as not everybody goes to a good school.

Tomorrow's outstanding schools need to develop an empirically robust methodology to go alongside any strategies aimed at securing equity. This sort of evidence is fundamental to effective professional practice (i.e. ensuring that strategies actually work). A classic example of this is the Education Endowment Foundation (EEF) Teaching and Learning Toolkit which offers evidence of the relative impact of strategies to close the gap, their trustworthiness, and their relative cost.[1]

This type of valid and reliable evidence base has long been the Achilles heel of managing change and innovation in education. The sort of interventions that current evidence would seem to point to as improving equity, and where further sustained research is necessary, might include:

- The development of language and social skills from birth.
- A focus on literacy in the family from birth.
- Targeted interventions to engage the most vulnerable learners.
- Community-based strategies designed to secure well-being – for example, focusing on parenting, diet, and psychological health.
- Opportunities for engagement in sport and the performing arts across the community.
- Community renewal schemes, including environmental projects.
- Support for vulnerable groups.
- Developing student leadership in all aspects of educational and community life.
- Schools openly and actively collaborating in cross-community projects.

There does seem to be a case for arguing that an explicit values system, derived from an ethical hegemony, is a fundamental component of any model of education because of its link to natural justice, the duty to act fairly and equitably, and also because of the possible relationship between a values consensus and strong academic performance. The example of Finland illustrates this:

> There is compelling clarity about and commitment to inclusive, equitable and innovative social values beyond as well as within the educational system. (Pont et al., 2009: 80)

The defining distinctiveness of education in Finland is probably explained through the related concepts of consensual authoritarianism and egalitarian conformity. Everybody knows, accepts, and

---

1   See https://educationendowmentfoundation.org.uk/resources/teaching-learning-toolkit.

acts on the 'right things'. In discussing the consistent success of the Finnish education system, Sahlberg (2011: 131) argues:

> Trusting schools and teachers is a consequence of a well-functioning civil society and high social capital. Honesty and trust ... are often seen as among the most basic values and the building blocks of Finnish society.

The outstanding school of tomorrow therefore has to engage in a constant internal dialogue about its own values as a community and then be active in working with its wider communities in securing consensus around key issues relevant to the education of young people. No decision taken in a school can ever be value-free. One of the most powerful attributes of such a school is moral confidence and clarity, based on the informed consent of community members. It is first and foremost a moral community, sharing a clear set of values, and working to embed them into the daily lives and experiences of every member. This view of the school has very real implications for leadership, participation, and voice.

To what extent does your school have elements of the following?

- A shared values system that is rooted in securing the entitlement to equity and excellence for all.
- School policies, strategies, and processes that are concerned with translating principle into practice and ensuring that the school's values are made concrete for every member of the school community.
- A commitment to inclusion, addressing disadvantage, and maximising the academic and personal potential of every individual through a focus on their well-being.
- Leadership focused on securing consistency and intervening in order to maximise the possibility of success in all aspects of educational outcomes.
- The ability to demonstrate the relationship between principle and practice.

Proposition 2

Tomorrow's outstanding school recognises that to secure equity it has to engage with the factors that are the most significant and influential in determining educational success and enhancing life chances. This means that it is actively engaged in securing positive outcomes in terms of family life, community, poverty, and social class, according to its context, even if these outcomes have an indirect impact over time.

Proposition 2 does not mean teachers become social workers, as some feel they are expected to be – a worrying cliché because, by definition, learning is a social process, so teachers and learners have to be *social* workers. What it does mean is that schools increasingly need to see the child in context and engage, as is necessary and appropriate, with the variables that are most likely to be amenable to change.

There is a significant political and conceptual debate about the relative significance and impact of social and contextual versus school-based variables. The school improvement perspective, which has dominated the last 20 or 30 years of thinking and practice, has tended to focus on the school itself as the primary source in the improvement of educational outcomes – for example, in terms of Ofsted ratings, performance at Key Stages 2 and 4 and examination performance at Key Stages 4 and 5. Alternative perspectives recognise the importance of the school but also place significant stress on socio-economic factors, arguing that in terms of well-being, life chances, and social success, it is these factors that will always outweigh, and often explain, the success of school-based approaches to securing equity. For example, as Desforges and Abouchaar (2003: 86) show, in the primary years the family is significantly more important than the school in terms of securing educational success.

Three broad conclusions emerge from Pont et al.'s (2009: 33) analysis of the factors influencing student learning. Firstly, student background characteristics – especially with regard to social, economic, and cultural background – frequently emerge as the most important source of variations in student achievement. Secondly, school-related factors, which are more open to policy influence, explain a smaller part of the variations in student learning than do student characteristics. Thirdly, amongst school-level variables, the factors that are closest to student learning, such as teacher quality and classroom practices, tend to have the strongest impact on student achievement.

From this perspective the overarching influence is a student's social context. School policies are important, but not as relatively significant as the quality of the classroom experience. This in turn is subordinate to social, cultural, and economic factors. Silins and Mulford (2002: 561–562) reinforce such a perspective when they state that: 'Most school effectiveness studies show that 80 per cent or more of student achievement can be explained by student background rather than schools.' This is broadly consistent with the case argued by Muijs (2010: 89) that:

> Even if we found all the factors that make schools more or less effective, we would still not be able to affect more than 30 percent of the variance in pupils' outcomes.

This leads us to a very clear conclusion:

> Schools can – and should – be charged with narrowing educational inequality. However, a focus on general school improvement policies will not be sufficient to do the job. (Clifton and Cook, 2012: 5)

The school is a significant variable and, in some respects, the most open to influence and change. However, the other key variables – poverty, social class, parenting, family life, and the quality of community engagement – can all be addressed with varying degrees of potential impact by schools

– *providing that* the role of the school is radically reappraised. According to the Audit Commission (2006: 4):

> Children's educational underachievement is linked with a wide range of deprivation factors: low parental qualifications, poor housing conditions, low family income, ill-health, family problems, and wider community factors such as low aspirations and unemployment.

Educational success in the school of tomorrow, however defined, will still be the result of the interaction of two key variables – social factors and school factors. The current consensus points to the social factors – parenting, community, social class, and poverty – being responsible for roughly 70–80% of the variables influencing academic success, well-being, and life chances. The school, by contrast, is only directly responsible for 20–30% of the factors influencing the outcomes (Silins and Mulford, 2002: 561; Moreno et al., 2007: 5). Note that there are some small, though relatively minor, variations in the relative percentage weights attached by different researchers.

Within schools, the greatest impact comes from the quality of teaching, with leadership directly contributing relatively little but being indirectly, through its influence on teaching, very significant. The scale of the challenge is exemplified in Figure 2, which illustrates the relationship between these factors.

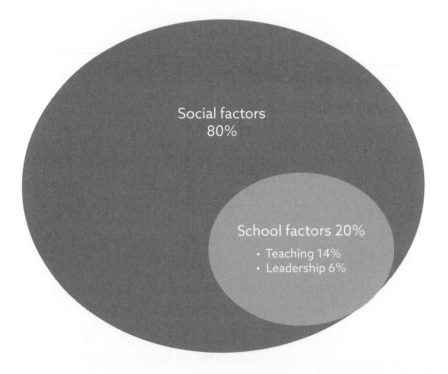

Figure 2: Relative influence of social and school factors on educational achievement

Another way to look at this is to consider the implications of the very simple fact that children spend roughly only 15% of their lives each year in school. Whilst that 15% is disproportionately significant it would be naive in the extreme to pretend that the school can function hermetically sealed from the community it serves. The 85% of time that students spend out of school is going to have an impact upon that 15%. The natural corollary of this division between school and non-school time is to recognise that learning is also distributed across a child's life in and out of school. It is equally fallacious to argue that 'You go to school to learn' or 'If you don't behave, you will not learn.' Children and young people are never not learning; they learn in every context, through every experience, and this needs to be recognised and respected in any proposition about schooling for tomorrow. The issue is what and how they learn.

So, tomorrow's outstanding school secures the 20–30% of factors that it directly controls by focusing on the quality of its provision. However, the school is also equally engaged in issues related to its socio-economic context with its families and communities. This perspective was reinforced by the Audit Commission (2006: 4–6) research report quoted on page 18.

If the family is significant, then so is the community. Putnam (2000: 296) is robust about the impact of the community as expressed through the concept of social capital:

> Child development is powerfully shaped by social capital ... trust, networks, and norms of reciprocity within a child's family, school, peer group, and larger community have wide-ranging effects on the child's opportunities and choices and, hence, on his behaviour and development.

Jerrim (2013: 3) demonstrates the very real impact of family and social advantage:

> High achieving boys from the most advantaged family backgrounds in England are roughly two and a half years ahead of their counterparts in the least advantaged households by the age of 15.

Morally, this is an issue at the heart of equity in education in a democratic society – high achievement in terms of academic criteria is very clearly correlated with family wealth. According to the Social Mobility and Child Poverty Commission (2013: 5):

- ... those in the most advantaged areas are still three times as likely to participate in higher education than those in the most disadvantaged areas.

- ... the most advantaged young people are seven times more likely to attend the most selective universities as the most disadvantaged.

- The odds of a child at a state secondary school who is eligible for free school meals in Year 11 being admitted to Oxbridge by the age of 19 is almost 2,000 to 1 against. By contrast, the odds of a privately educated child being admitted to Oxbridge are 20 to 1.

It might be that, as appropriate, the outstanding school of tomorrow actively engages with the 70–80% of factors traditionally considered beyond their influence in order to move towards equity and to close the various gaps that compromise the potential of children and young people.

To what extent does your school have elements of the following?

- A focus on ensuring that the 20–30% of factors the school does control are working to optimum effect.
- A vision of effective learning and academic success as the result of partnerships involving vertical integration (early years to higher education) and horizontal integration (family, community, and other services).
- A move towards establishing the school itself as a model of an effective community.
- An active role in developing leadership capacity across its communities, especially with students.
- A focus on establishing school leaders as social entrepreneurs, developing social capital through projects that have the potential to enhance the communities within the school's orbit.

Proposition 3

Learning is a social experience rooted in family, community, and school that can only be considered outstanding in the extent to which it is both personalised and rooted in authentic social relationships.

The dominant and pervasive model of schooling is essentially one of engagement with subjects. This is rather bizarre, as it is only schools, and secondary schools in particular, along with higher education institutions, that are actually concerned with subjects. The vast majority of people do not 'do' maths or science in this discrete sense. They solve problems, make decisions, and work closely with others in doing so, albeit, and importantly, drawing on both mathematical or scientific knowledge and skills. Only in education is working with another person seen as cheating – for most adults it is a requirement of their work. If one of the functions of schooling is to prepare young people for adult life, then leading a school of tomorrow will mean developing a very different approach to the curriculum and to teaching and learning.

By any set of criteria, the world that young people will inherit will be one of great complexity and challenge, and we will examine this in some detail in Chapter 3. The potential issues emerging from climate change, population growth, political extremism, and the demands of an increasingly heterogeneous society all point to the inadequacy of relying solely on traditional models of teaching and learning. Tomorrow's outstanding school will therefore be less concerned with the teaching of subjects in isolation and more concerned with learning how to apply subject knowledge in collaboration with others.

This is not to neglect or diminish the importance of subject knowledge but rather to see it as a means, not as an end, and to shift the emphasis of schooling on to acquiring the discipline of the subject, not just the diluted information – that is, developing the intellectual skills of, *inter alia*, analysis, explanation, justification, and synthesis. This implies a very different perspective on learning. In essence, the school of tomorrow starts with learning, and the curriculum and teaching are derived from what we know about what successful learning is for every learner. This in turn suggests that in the future schools will function around a set of propositions about learning rather than about teaching – whereas it is the teaching of the curriculum rather than the learning of students that currently drives many school timetables.

A possible range of propositions about such learning might include:

- Every learner is unique – every learner has a unique personal profile in terms of literacy, stage of cognitive development, intrinsic motivation and ambition, preferred learning strategies, and personal needs. This complex set of variables can only be properly responded to through a strategy based on personalised pathways that respond to the needs and dignity of the individual learner.

- Learning is a social process – this points to the development of personal, interpersonal, and community-based behaviours and strategies that create effective learning environments. In particular, it highlights learning as a collaborative process.

- Intelligence can be learned – cognitive potential is not fixed at birth (nature), nor is it solely the product of environment (nurture); rather nature can be influenced via nurture.

- Cognitive interventions – the skills-based curriculum – can enhance the possibility of equity by developing skills and strategies that may not always be available through the learner's social context. This is particularly true of literacy and a range of higher order cognitive behaviours.

- Learning can take place anytime, anywhere, with anyone – this means according far greater status and significance to learning in the family, with peers, and across the community. Most students spend around 15% of their lives in school. For the remaining 85% of the time, when they are awake, they need to be engaged in a range of personal, family, peer, and community-based learning opportunities, such as sport, music, drama, community projects, and also having fun. Additionally, we need to recognise that some of these communities may be online ones.

- The purpose of teaching is to enable learning – this implies the role of the teacher as coach, mentor, facilitator, and scaffolder. It also points to the range of possible learning relationships in which the whole community is actively engaged in reciprocal teaching and learning.

- For a very small proportion of people, particularly teachers in schools and in higher education, academic subjects are fundamental to their professional growth and credibility. For everybody else they are part of a personal portfolio of knowledge, skills, and qualities. The school of the future has a core curriculum centred on skills – literacy, numeracy, relationships, thinking and reasoning, and ICT. These are developed through a sequence of learning relationships rooted in the family and community.

To what extent does your school recognise elements of the following?

- Effective learning starts with the individual and has to be differentiated according to each learner's distinctive identity.
- Learning has to be based on stage rather than age.
- In the final analysis, the curriculum is the totality of a learner's educational experiences.
- Quality teaching is significantly influenced by relationships with peers and adults, and these need to be explicitly addressed in terms of skills and behaviours through appropriate modelling, coaching, and strategies such as Philosophy for Children.
- Teachers create multiple social learning opportunities that recognise the importance of play and social interaction.

Proposition 4

Leadership for the school of tomorrow must be seen in terms of collective capacity rather than personal hierarchical status. Leadership is a resource to be developed as and when it is needed, irrespective of the age, status, or formal role of the leaders. Equally, leadership needs to be seen in terms of leading a community rather than an organisation, and in terms of collaborative relationships.

One of the most significant challenges in rethinking the fundamental assumptions underpinning the theory and practice of contemporary education is the question of the appropriateness of hierarchical models. There are numerous permutations of hierarchy found in education – the differentiated status of teachers according to the age of their pupils, the relative significance of primary and secondary schools in terms of funding, the management structure of most schools, and the content and nature of the curriculum, in which some subjects are accorded greater significance than others in terms of time and resources.

This takes us on to the long-established proposition that EQ (or emotional intelligence) is more important than IQ (intelligence quotient) as a predictor of success; that, in fact, social relationships are the single most important determinant of success in any human endeavour (Goleman, 1995). From an educational perspective, learning how is at least as significant as learning what, and the foundation of the how has always been the quality of the social interaction in the classroom.

Of course, there is always a place for the recluse and the misanthrope, but in the context of effective learning the quality of social relationships is a defining criterion in terms of the potential for successful outcomes. One way of understanding our potential to engage is by applying aspects of the idea of social capital usually described as bonding and bridging (Field, 2008: 36). In essence, bonding is essentially introvert and exclusive – focusing on the internal needs of the school and its stakeholders; bridging is extrovert, inclusive, and engaging – looking outside the school gates and considering the mutual benefits of external relationships. Thus, some schools will actively seek to develop partnerships with other schools, sharing professional development activities and working collaboratively on school improvement projects. There are equally schools that will stand aloof from any type of interaction with other schools. There is a challenge in managing the ratio between the two in any social organisation, but particularly in a school.

A logical corollary of bridging-based approaches is that leadership is seen as 'lateral' rather than 'vertical'. In other words, the school has to move from the historical approach of top-down hierarchy to a more appropriate approach based on collective capacity. That means leadership is available to all, and is a shared resource, accessed as appropriate. In practical terms this means that, irrespective of age or relative status, individuals are able to lead in appropriate ways according to ability rather than seniority.

The challenges inherent in moving from a culture rooted in bonding, essentially the territorial imperative, to a culture rooted in bridging are substantial. The history and governance of schools reinforce the idea of institutional autonomy as the norm. Movement towards a competition-driven market economy can only reinforce this dominant perspective. Of course, the move to a MAT-based system poses similar challenges at a trust level, whilst the balance of autonomy and interdependence between constituent schools inevitably adds a new twist, and we will explore this further in Chapter 9.

Leadership in the school of tomorrow, either in the context of an individual school or MAT, therefore has to model a range of behaviours to reinforce collaboration and mutual interdependence:

- Using open dialogue, personal, and community conversations to articulate, define, explain, justify, and exemplify the moral foundations of the community and its partnerships.
- Embedding learning processes at the heart of every role, strategy, and policy.
- Working through targeted interventions and projects designed to focus energy, resources, and commitment towards securing equity.
- Building capacity and sustainability through systematic succession planning and leadership development across the community.
- Developing a high-trust community through an explicit focus on quality relationships.
- Building rich networks.
- Focusing on collective and personal well-being.

To what extent does your school have elements of the following?

- A perception of the centrality of trust as a component of organisational life and as a quality of leaders.
- A vision of collaboration as the defining quality of organisational success and the basis of all key working procedures and relationships.
- A focus on building bridges across the school and with other schools.
- Deliberate and systematic approaches towards building bridges with parents and the wider community.
- A vision of leadership as creating and nurturing networks.

School leaders who understand the need to inhabit the second horizon between today and tomorrow will need to translate these values and principles into outstanding learning for all children and young people. However, they will have to do so within a complex and contradictory context. In Chapter 2 we explore what we see as some of the key contradictions which have to be faced within the current policy environment in England. Then in Chapter 3 we will balance this with an examination of the emerging global trends that to some degree will shape the tomorrows of us all.

Questions for reflection and discussion

- How confident are you that your curriculum model is based on a holistic and inclusive view of learning that includes the wider issue of well-being and respects the dignity and entitlement of all learners?
- To what extent does your leadership help to secure equity for the community your school serves?
- In what ways are families and the wider community integrated into the educational aspects of the school's life?
- To what extent is your school an authentically collaborative community? How do you know?

Chapter 2

Tensions and Contradictions: Five Major Challenges School Leaders Face Today

This chapter is rooted firmly in today and in the world of the first horizon. It attempts to map the key systemic issues facing all school leaders in the short to medium term in a climate of unprecedented upheaval. It explores five inherent tensions with which leaders working within the second horizon must inevitably still grapple as they seek to build on and apply the four principles we articulated in Chapter 1.

The changing policy context in England

In the decades following the 1944 Education Act, education policy was largely directed by a socially democratic, one nation perspective, with a very significant consensus around the core purpose of education – to reduce social inequality in order to create equality of opportunity. The education system operated between national government, local government, and schools, in a sometimes tense relationship, with a fairly clear and consistent division of labour. In essence, national government set strategic policy, which was interpreted and applied by local government, with schools having significant influence over the core matters of pedagogy and curriculum.

This largely consensual relationship – based on a high degree of mutual tolerance and acceptance – was fundamentally challenged by Labour Prime Minister James Callaghan's 1976 Ruskin College speech, in which he questioned the prevailing orthodoxy and, in effect, opened the gates of the 'secret garden' of the curriculum. This led to a paradoxical period in education policy-making, which still persists, with all sorts of integral contradictions and anomalies with which leaders who are mindful of tomorrow nevertheless have to wrestle today. It is worth noting that these dubious policies do not fall on just one side of the simplistic traditional divide of left and right. Moreover, we do not suggest that in the main they are caused by malice, ignorance, or incompetence on the part of policy-makers. We seek to argue that the tensions and difficulties are caused because, at root, policy is trying to patch up a flawed and broken model. It is constrained because of thinking which is constructed purely in terms of the first horizon.

In talking about a broken model of schooling, you could be forgiven for construing this as an argument for yet more structural reform. However, nothing could be further from the truth. Rather, we argue that the problem is not with structures per se, but with outmoded and limited views as to what constitutes purpose and quality in schooling. Equally, this is not a criticism of those who work in the present system and devote extraordinary effort to trying to do the best they possibly can within those constraints.

The most significant consideration, and the one that underpins this chapter, as in Chapter 1, is the issue of equity in education and, particularly, the need to develop strategies that actually address this issue. What is very clear is that developing alternative structural models does little, if anything, to impact on the actual level of performance of the education system. Firstly, consider the number of structural changes that have taken place over the last 10 years in the education system in England. Then consider the impact they have had on school performance from the following perspectives:

> Although four out of five children now achieve the expected standards at primary school, one in five still does not, and around two in five young people leave secondary school without five or more A*-C GCSEs or equivalents including English and Maths. Poor children still have worse educational outcomes at every stage and we have a long tail of low attainment. (Department for Education, 2016: 6)

> The attainment gap between FSM and non-FSM secondary students hasn't budged in a decade. It was 28 percentage points 10 years ago and it is still 28 percentage points today. Thousands of poor children who are in the top 10% nationally at age 11 do not make it into the top 25% five years later. (Wilshaw, 2016)

> The average science, mathematics and reading scores of pupils in England have not changed since 2006. The average science score in England has remained consistent since 2006 and is higher than the average score of 15-year-olds in 52 countries. The average mathematics score for England has remained stable since 2006. As is the case with science and mathematics, there is no evidence of a significant change in average reading scores in England since 2006. (Jerrim and Shure, 2016: 4)

Over this same period the number of schools that are either good or outstanding, according to Ofsted criteria, has risen to 86% (Ofsted, 2016: 5), and performance at both Key Stage 2 and Key Stage 4 has improved. But the gap in the performance of free school meal (FSM) and non-free school meal (non-FSM) pupils has not closed. In fact, it has widened. And the gap is actually wider in outstanding secondary schools than in schools requiring improvement.

The dilemma facing successive secretaries of state for education has been their inability to find the magic wand that secures the optimum outcome of both sustaining improvement *and* closing the gap. Apart from a brief foray under New Labour, manifested in the various elements of Every Child Matters, reform interventions have been almost exclusively focused on the school – in essence, school improvement in various guises. The various strategies have been school-centric rather than focused on the development of social justice, in the sense of social fairness and equity more broadly, in spite of the messages from high performing education systems that improving educational performance is a function of social well-being and economic security. Rather, social policy has moved in the general direction of a neo-liberal approach:

> The political New Right represents a coalition of neo-liberal and neo-conservative thinking. The former promotes the virtue of a free-market economy as a more effective mechanism for the distribution of social resources, competition, privatization and individual liberty, while the latter privileges tradition, hierarchy, authority and social order. (Garratt and Forrester, 2012: 10)

Education policy-making has shown a steady drift since the advent of the Blair government in 1997 towards essentially neo-liberal policies which might be defined and compared using the perspectives outlined in Figure 3.

A model like this inevitably creates artificial boundaries and over-simple definitions. Underpinning any such analysis is a range of assumptions. Much of the discussion in this chapter is based on the premise that the nature of a public service such as education has certain key characteristics. Pring (2013: 154) argues that a public service has four defining components: it is available to all; it is universal in application; choices are made in the interests of the client, not the provider; and it is publicly accountable through democratic processes.

With that in mind, let us examine each of the five areas of tension identified in Figure 3 in turn.

1. Devolution versus centralisation

In many ways, the recent history of education policy might be seen as a balancing act between delegating to schools and enhancing central control, often at the same time. This is the essential paradox confronting school leadership and governance – competing and contradictory imperatives. A classic example is the Education Reform Act 1988 that led to changes across the 1990s, notably the introduction of the national curriculum, which tightened control over what was taught in schools, partnered with the introduction of local management of schools (LMS), grant-maintained schools, and, eventually, academies, which then loosened central control and effectively eliminated local government's involvement in the key activities of educational policy and practice

This is part of a process that is often characterised as balancing loose–tight relationships (Peters and Waterman, 2015). One of the identified characteristics of high performing, excellent businesses in the United States in the 1980s was their ability to reconcile these imperatives – that is, to be able to balance that which is tight, non-negotiable, and subject to control with that which is loose, negotiable, and open to delegation and devolution of authority and control. Effective management and leadership, it was argued, was skilful in achieving an appropriate balance, both in terms of what was devolved and to whom. Increased devolution was generally interpreted as an opportunity to move organisations towards what is often described as managerialism, where means, structures, and policies become more important than purpose:

> A range of approaches to site-based management supported shifts in professional practice away from the classroom towards budgets, marketing, human resources and organizational culture. (Gunter, 2016: 151)

Focus	Neo-liberal/ neo-conservative perspectives	Socially democratic perspectives	Resulting tensions
The nature of society	Competition is the norm in personal, social, and economic relationships. The state should not interfere in the free market.	The state has a duty to intervene to secure equity and social justice.	Devolution versus centralisation
The nature of an education system	To develop a culture of performativity and accountability. To compete for pupils but to collaborate in order to improve.	To facilitate a self-improving school system (e.g. teaching school alliances (TSAs)).	Independence versus collaboration
The role of government	To hold schools to account (Ofsted) and intervene if underperforming (e.g. regional schools commissioners (RSCs)).	To initiate intervention strategies (e.g. Every Child Matters). To support schools through the provision of services and agencies (e.g. NCTL).	Professionalism versus accountability
The role of schools	To provide cost-effective education.	To help secure equity (e.g. the pupil premium).	Doing more with less
The purpose of education	To reinforce prevailing social norms and values. To educate the future workforce. To embed social conventions.	Combining academic success with personal development and well-being.	Measurement and value

Figure 3: Areas of tension arising from neo-liberal/ neo-conservative and socially democratic perspectives

Education policy in England in the late 1980s and 1990s saw movement towards devolution, but, significantly, perhaps the balance of tight and loose was the wrong way round. In essence, responsibility for finance was devolved under the LMS scheme, but responsibility for the curriculum was centralised and tightened, starting with the national curriculum and culminating in introduction of the literacy hour.

The experience in many organisations was quite the reverse – a high degree of centralisation with regard to finance but a great deal of openness and high trust with regard to the development of new products or innovations in processes. A classic example is the near demise and triumphant revival of the LEGO organisation. The recovery was based on two parallel strategies – financial rigour and customer focus. So costs were cut and financial disciplines were introduced. At the same time senior managers sought the participation of a range of different groups who had the potential to influence from both inside and outside the business and looked to recruit a diverse and creative staff. It tried to create new products that disrupted existing markets, and it listened to customer feedback. The company employs LEGO enthusiasts to play and develop new products – but then employs a rigorous discipline in terms of product development, cost control, and profitability (Robertson and Breen, 2013).

One of the key themes of the total quality management (TQM) methodology, which was popular in industry in the late 1980s and 1990s, was the need to develop self-managing teams who took on responsibility for maintaining quality in all aspects of organisational culture, whether that be in the manufacturing process or in levels of customer service. Schools explored the possibilities of this management system, which largely explained the post-war Japanese economic miracle, and many adopted and modified a range of strategies including the use of mission statements to focus on corporate values, the centrality of teams and quality relationships, obtaining feedback, and recognising the importance of customer feedback and satisfaction (West-Burnham, 1997).

It therefore seems perverse that schools had to develop systems, strategies, and skills to manage finance, perhaps not their natural forte, whilst losing control over areas of expertise aligned with their core purpose. The same incongruity can be found in the movement from clinical to managerial control in the NHS in the UK.

What is most significant about this uneasy balance of devolution, which has been a key element in education policy for the past generation of teachers and school leaders, is that it has had virtually no direct impact on the performance of the education system, in spite of the commitment to close the gap and raise standards. As we have argued, the performance of the education system, by a range of measures, has remained stubbornly resistant to policy interventions. Neither does the legal status of academies as state-funded independent schools, usually working through MATs, appear to be having a significant impact on outcomes or economic effectiveness across the whole system (Benn and Downs, 2015: 76). Some MATs have been highly successful in raising standards, so were some local authorities (LAs); equally some MATs have not been successful – as with some LAs.

The question of funding and efficiency in education is certainly not a new concern. In 1862, Robert Lowe recommended his Revised Code to the House of Commons with a caveat (quoted in Sylvester,

1974: 61) about his proposed new system: 'If it is not cheap it shall be efficient; if it is not efficient it shall be cheap.' He was speaking to a House whose members were unfamiliar with the existing school system and to whom, arguably, cheapness was more important than efficiency. Lowe himself recognised that a system cannot be both efficient and cheap, but that we should not begrudge investment if it achieves greater measurable outcomes. He saw the need for national thrift and, as a Benthamite wedded to calculation, recognised that the quantified results of examinations in the three Rs were a more precise measure than the qualitative comments of inspectors in assessing the efficiency of schools. In many respects, very little has changed today.

2. Independence versus collaboration

Any model of organisational structure, whether at an international, governmental, or business level, will have at its heart the crucial relationship between the parts and the whole. This could operate on many different levels, including that of federal or unitary states, international alliances such as the European Union, multinational companies, businesses with multiple branches, and also includes the relationship between the individual and the organisation. The key concept we need to apply to our understanding of these relationships is the notion of subsidiarity, which means that decisions are taken at the most appropriate level.

Subsidiarity is the principle that a larger and more complex organisation should only perform those tasks which cannot be carried out as well by a smaller and simpler organisation. In other words, any activity which can be performed by a more decentralised entity should be. It is a bulwark designed to protect personal freedom and diffuse centralised control, and it directly conflicts with the passion for centralisation and bureaucracy characteristic of corporate states. Subsidiarity is one of the key values underpinning federal states where certain functions are reserved under the jurisdiction of the constituent states and others are the responsibility of the federal government – usually defence and foreign affairs.

There is potentially a fundamental tension between personal and organisational autonomy or in the varying degrees of collaboration and centralised control. This is exacerbated in the British system because of some deep cultural norms surrounding the concept of the professional teacher, the (largely mythical) autonomy of the head teacher, and the very strong sense of the autonomous school.

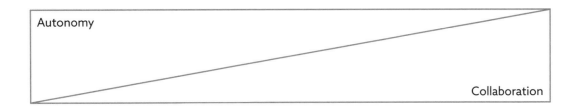

Figure 4: The balance of autonomy and collaboration

For the education profession, norms and expectations would tend to be exemplified by the left-hand side of Figure 4. What might be characterised as the 'my classroom' and 'my school' culture assumes that autonomy is the basis of organisational relationships. This is sometimes manifested in large schools as the Balkanisation of subject departments or pastoral structures. Even in the primary school this can be seen in the distinctive culture of phase teams. The presumption of autonomy can serve to inhibit if not actually compromise the potential for collaboration, which evidently raises some significant challenges for the prevailing orthodoxy, if we accept collaboration as an essential component of a self-improving school system.

Historically, collaboration has been largely ad hoc and either short-term or purely functional. In a speech at the ASCL annual conference in March 2016, Sir David Carter, the national schools commissioner, was very clear about the future shape of the education system and its implications for teachers, school leaders, and governors. In answer to the question, 'Does membership of a MAT reduce autonomy?' his response was, 'Yes, it probably does!'

Sir David identified the areas in which, in his view, collaboration is necessary to secure entitlement to the best education possible:

- Systems and operating procedures
- Data collection points
- Common exam syllabi
- Assessment and reporting
- Key educational policies
- HR practice as one employer

He also identified areas where he felt some degree of autonomy would remain:

- Culture of the school
- Uniform
- Enrichment
- Relationship with the local community
- Educational networks unique to the school

There is an obvious potential tension between the collaborative approach that enables the development of high quality, consistent working policies and practices and the traditional, autonomous modes of operating:

> In the old days, and still too much today, the professional culture of teaching was one of individual classroom autonomy, unquestioned experience, and unassailable knowledge and expertise. Nowadays, professional cultures are more and more collaborative. (Hargreaves and Fullan, 2012: 143)

3. Professionalism versus accountability

The debate about whether teachers are afforded professional status is in one sense somewhat arcane and only marginal to their actual daily lives.

The essential criteria for professional status are usually taken to be:

- Entry to the profession is controlled – i.e. the profession sets academic entry standards and decides on the suitability of applicants.
- The profession defines the ethical basis of professional practice and adjudicates on breaches of such practice – i.e. the profession is self-regulating.
- Professionals work in the public interest and for the common good – in certain contexts professionalism may imply altruistic behaviour.
- Professional bodies define and implement the standards of expertise and knowledge necessary to practice.
- Individuals work to the most exacting professional standards based in reciprocal trust.
- The profession controls a body that is authoritative in all matters listed above.

Obvious examples of professions that meet these criteria are the law and medicine, but education doesn't strictly conform. For many doctors the principles of the Hippocratic Oath, notably 'do no harm', form the basis of their practice. Lawyers are bound by the duties of an officer of the court – that is, an obligation to promote justice and the effective working of the legal system. There are no real equivalents in education, and it is probably fair to say that the Teachers' Standards are not central to educators' practice.

Chosen criteria could demonstrate that teachers either are or – as demonstrated above – are not professional. If the argument is so open-ended, you might be wondering why it is worthy of note. Whether we think of teaching as a profession or not hinges on the relative significance attached to a range of criteria, and is usually resolved by subjective judgement. This is what makes the debate, in fact, fundamental as it reveals a range of key assumptions about how education actually works. One way of resolving what is an increasingly circular debate is to abandon the emphasis on fixed criteria and focus instead on practice – *professionalism* rather than professional status. Teachers are professionals in that they act with professionalism, not according to how far they meet a range of criteria that are never going to be fully available to employees of publicly funded institutions.

Comparisons between various occupational groups in terms of workload or public esteem are invidious. What is clear is that successive governments have resisted attempts at what might be described as professional autonomy in education, perhaps simply on the basis of the numbers involved – the vast majority of teachers are public employees or are employed by publicly funded trusts. If teachers were professionally autonomous then they would determine the curriculum and set standards of teaching and learning – very much as they do in Finland. The debate about teaching as a profession will almost always be essentially circular and, in many respects, does not have a significant impact on most of the practical, day-to-day issues facing schools, apart from when it comes to the issue of accountability, but it remains a significant issue in terms of the way in which educationalists are perceived and perceive themselves.

Professions, according to the criteria outlined, tend to set their own moral standards and adjudicate on breaches of those standards. Teachers, on the other hand, are subject to externally imposed standards of accountability. However, this does not preclude a genuine and rigorous sense of moral duty and responsibility. What is very clear is the extent to which most teachers, school leaders, and governors embrace the principles of professionalism, which might be best understood in the following terms:

- Accepting that educating young people is an essentially moral activity that carries clear duties and responsibilities.
- Working to secure social justice and equity.
- Having a clear duty of care and responsibility for safeguarding.
- Working to high standards of quality and service with a high degree of personal authority expressed through trust.

However, the rhetoric of valuing teachers' professionalism is contradicted by the existence of the Ofsted process and other models of external accountability – whereas other professions are self-monitoring; they manage poor performance, and reward good performance, themselves. The Ofsted inspection process and the emerging role of regional schools commissioners in forming judgements about the success, or otherwise, of schools are both largely expressions of performativity.

There seems to be a high correlation between the performance of a school or trust and the tenure of the principal, head teacher, or CEO. Yet this goes directly against what we know about some of the highest performing education systems in the world. It does seem to be the case that a culture of high regard and trust is directly aligned with high performance:

> A typical feature of teaching and learning in Finland is high confidence in teachers and principals regarding curriculum, assessment, organization of teaching, and evaluation of the work of the school ... What is important is that today's Finnish education policies are a result of 3 decades of systematic, mostly intentional development that has created a culture of diversity, trust, and respect. (Sahlberg, 2015: 152–153)

Finland, along with other high-trust societies such as the Netherlands, achieves high performance without performativity through the respect that comes from recognising the moral basis of professionalism, which in turn engenders trust and so reinforces performance. This perspective is reinforced by Bryk and his colleagues in their study of Chicago schools:

> Through their actions, school participants articulate their sense of obligation toward others, and others in turn come to discern the intentionality enacted here ... Even simple interactions, if successful, can enhance capacities for more complex subsequent actions. In this regard, increasing trust and productive organizational changes reciprocate each other. (Bryk et al., 2010: 139)

In essence, the culture of Finnish society, and in the schools in Bryk's research, points to the very simple proposition that high trust equals high performance. In certain crucial respects English society is essentially low trust, and this has a negative impact right the way through the education system. High-trust societies tend not to have high-stakes accountability models, such as Ofsted, or a national curriculum. They do not publish league tables. Externally driven, high-stakes accountability results in internal high-stakes accountability, and so the culture of performativity becomes more deeply embedded. Spend time in any Year 6 or Year 11 class to see the effect of internal high-stakes accountability.

4. Doing more with less

Growth in the national level of per-pupil spending on schooling has varied over time: rising during the 1980s, freezing during the 1990s, growing fast during the 2000s, and slowing down since 2010. The current generation of school leaders and governors have generally worked in a context of growth averaging 5% in the 2000s and 1% since (Belfield and Sibieta, 2016: 2).

Policy priorities have also shifted funding, with the creation, in the 2000s, of specific grants targeted at the most deprived schools as part of the government's Every Child Matters strategies, a trend continued with the introduction of the pupil premium in 2011. At the same time, demographics have also changed, particularly the number of school-age children, which fell over much of the first decade of the twenty-first century and is now rising again at a rapid rate (Institute for Fiscal Studies, 2015). Some school budgets will grow significantly given a rise in pupil numbers and an increase in the number of children who qualify to receive the pupil premium.

However, the Institute for Fiscal Studies (2017) has indicated that, by 2016 projections, there could be a real-term reduction in some school budgets of 7% per child after 2020. When the extra costs of teachers' pensions, national insurance contributions, and wage increases are included, the real-term reduction in spending could be closer to 12%.

The net result of this is that school leaders and governors need to move from a mindset based on financial growth to one based on economies and constraints, and, in particular, to begin to explore potential savings, economies of scale, and a culture of 'more for less' – best manifested in concepts related to cost-effectiveness, value for money, and the relationship between expenditure and impact.

Cost-benefit analysis is widely used in a range of contexts. For example, in health it is used by the National Institute for Health and Care Excellence (NICE) to determine whether the cost of a new drug or procedure is justified in terms of the impact on patients' health and well-being. In an educational context, the best-known example of a cost-benefit analysis approach is the EEF Teaching and Learning Toolkit (as discussed on page 15). The purpose of the toolkit is to provide evidence in order to support decisions around the most effective use of the pupil premium. When first published the conclusions of the analysis were highly controversial, largely because they challenged professional intuition – for example, that smaller class sizes and more adults in the classroom would be better in terms of outcomes. Both are undoubtedly desirable from many other perspectives, but they demonstrate relatively limited impact on actual attainment. The highest impact strategies – feedback, metacognitive development, homework in the secondary school, and mastery learning reinforced by collaborative approaches – should, at least in theory, be the basis for most schools' approaches to working with pupil premium pupils (even though we use the term with some distaste for this blanket labelling of pupils).

An evaluation of the use of pupil premium funding (Cunningham and Lewis, 2012: 6) found that the most commonly used strategies included early intervention schemes, reduced class sizes, more one-to-one tuition, and additional teaching assistants – all of which are problematic from a cost-benefit approach. In the survey, just over half (52%) of the teachers said their school used past experience of what works to decide which approaches and programmes to adopt to improve pupils' learning. However, the number saying their school used research evidence to make these decisions was only just over a third (36%).

'More for less' implies a movement in schools and MATs towards financial strategies that use objective, evidence-based approaches – approaches based on criteria derived from explicit values and educational priorities. This might involve exploring a range of options which are not part of the usual repertoire of resource management in schools, such as:

- Collaborative working to optimise the potential for economies of scale.
- Alternative models of staffing in order to maximise the quality of teaching and performance through flexibility in deployment.
- Exploring the potential to economise through the effective use of ICT.

5. Measurement and value

It is one of the great clichés of recent years and yet it remains profoundly true: 'We must learn to measure what we value rather than valuing what we can easily measure' (Education Counts: Report to the US Congress 1991, quoted by MacBeath, 2006: 64). This takes us to the very heart of the tension between neo-liberal perspectives and democratic models of social engagement. Central to the debate about measurement and value are the issues of what is to be measured and how. Clearly there has to be some form of measurement that allows for the identification of success. However, this should not be done in such a way as to distort the educational process – for instance, as key stage testing totally distorts the curriculum in Years 6, 10, and 11.

A major problem is that there is no real consensus in most systems as to what the purpose and nature of education should be. Most systems have permutations of some or most of the following aims:

- Passing on social values and norms to the next generation.
- Achieving social justice through equity.
- Supporting the development of personal well-being.
- Securing the entitlement to basic education.
- Supporting the development of academic potential.
- Developing citizens and members of communities.
- Securing employability.
- Nurturing talent and giftedness.

What is challenging about this list is achieving the precise balance between these various components – what are the ideal respective ratios, and how should the ingredients be blended? It is this balance, and the system of measurement, that determines the nature of the learning experience in schools and across communities.

As far as measurement is concerned, one of the key tensions in the social sciences is in the relationship between the quantitative and the qualitative. There is a tendency to ascribe greater validity, reliability, and trustworthiness to the numerical rather than the arguably subjective: it is argued that mathematical data is more objective and reliable than narrative descriptions of personal experience and opinions. There has long been a tension in educational assessment between whether to measure outcomes by purely quantitative criteria or by an alternative, interpretivist perspective, which is essentially subjective. In some ways, the history of education could be conceptualised as the tension between a Gradgrindian perspective based on facts and a Rousseauian view concerned with perceptions and insights. As is so often the case, the ideal probably lies between the two, but the failure to recognise the different merits of each leads to fundamental misunderstandings.

In medical practice, a clinical diagnosis will usually be based on a wide range of data, including objective and quantifiable measurements (e.g. blood pressure or heart rate), clinical investigations (e.g. CAT scan or X-ray) and responses from the patient (e.g. their description of their symptoms, medical history, and so on). The combination of information yielded hopefully results in a successful and accurate diagnosis and so treatment. However, there is another element to the diagnostic process, and that is the knowledge, expertise, and intuition of the professional. For example, a highly experienced doctor will have an intuitive response to a patient's symptoms which suggests a likely diagnosis.

We can envisage these types of measurement as a spectrum (Figure 5): at the objective end might be hard science that is virtually incontrovertible (e.g. DNA testing) or the scientifically rigorous randomised controlled trial; and at the subjective end might be intuitive or anecdotal evidence, hearsay, and gossip. It is important to respect experience, wisdom, and insight and achieve a balance of approaches appropriate to the topic under review. At the same time, it is important not to defer to the tyranny of experience or the attraction of the anecdotal.

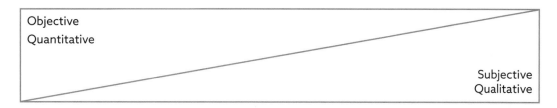

Objective
Quantitative

Subjective
Qualitative

Figure 5: Balancing objective and subjective factors in measurement

There is a complex relationship between the culture of assessment at a system level and at an institutional level: the system sees assessment as a measure of accountability, but to the school, assessment is a crucial element in the learning process itself. If the prevailing culture of accountability is based on performativity, then the chances are that assessment for learning will also come to focus on these notions of performance, however reductionist, instrumental, or inappropriate.

The practical implication would seem to be that the mode of assessment and accountability will become the dominant influence on both the content of the curriculum and the strategies for teaching and learning – the assessment tail wagging the education dog.

Pring (2013: 79) argues that there is a danger that assessment for accountability might contaminate assessment for learning:

> An essential distinction is between *assessment for learning* (AfL) and *assessment for accountability* – a distinction that policy makers do not seem able to grasp ... Assessment for accountability usually gives the overall performance of a school system or a school.

Whereas in Pring's (2013: 79) view, assessment for learning is 'the process of seeking and interpreting evidence for use by learners and their teachers'. This cross-contamination has of course happened, and a preoccupation with grade-giving is usually justified on the grounds that 'parents can understand it' – that is, it is free of educational jargon and presents data in a straightforward way. Much of current thinking assumes an integrity and veracity in educational statistics that we now know may not always be justified. There is a chasm between the criteria appropriate to judging schools and the criteria necessary to inform progress as a learner. As Pring (2013: 80) puts it: 'such tests and measures can never capture the subtlety of young people's learning'. There is a need to develop criteria and means of measurement that reflect the totality of an educational experience, not just comparative performance in a limited number of academic subjects.

Those school leaders who are building their planes as they fly have no choice but to navigate a way through these tensions and contradictions in public discourse and government policy. These tensions are not going to disappear in the short to medium term, even though they may come under increasing scrutiny as the limitations of current thinking about school purpose and quality become more apparent. It is unlikely that there will suddenly be some earmarked pot of new funding to develop the schools of tomorrow, nor is that necessarily needed, welcome as appropriate levels of funding clearly are. Neither is it a matter of waiting for further imposed structural reform to make creating the school of the future possible. Waiting is not an option and it is not likely to help.

Fundamentally we are arguing for a broader view of school purpose and quality, around which school leaders need to build an informed commitment by engaging differently with local stakeholders. Such a view is rooted in a clear set of ethical principles and values (outlined in Chapter 1); you may find it useful to regularly remind yourself of our four propositions as you reflect on the evidence and argument we present throughout the book.

In this chapter we have seen how school leaders today have to struggle constantly with policies and circumstances that represent a number of inherent tensions. For example, an increase in socio-economic inequality means that educational inequity also increases; the Ofsted accountability framework means reduced respect towards and trust in teachers, particularly in schools in challenging circumstances; the focus on attainment has detracted from a more holistic perspective of individual development and well-being (despite recent recognition of the importance of character and well-being); the emphasis on factors for improvement which are within schools' control has resulted in a disconnect from the communities within which they are situated. The school leaders we will introduce to you in Part Two accept these tensions and work within them, recognising that the conflicts, and the competing political demands from which they spring, have to be acknowledged and given their place. Leaders working on the second horizon attach a suitably restrained importance to them and recognise that they should not be considered of overriding significance.

However, our position is equally informed by a keen awareness of how the wider world in which schools function – and in which children and young people are growing up – is changing, and is likely to change exponentially in the foreseeable future. This brings a whole other dimension into play in our attempts to refocus our understanding of purpose and quality in schooling, and forms the theme of Chapter 3.

Questions for reflection and discussion

- How comfortable are you in reconciling competition and collaboration? Where do your professional instincts point?
- What should be the role of central government in education? On what basis should schools be held accountable and how? What part should trust play?
- How do you strike a balance in your curriculum between thinking in terms of social usefulness and employability – essentially a reductionist approach – or thinking about the development of the whole child?
- How should we measure educational success?

Chapter 3

A World of Change: Ten Major Global Trends That Challenge Our Conceptions of Education and Learning

The future ain't what it used to be.

attributed to Yogi Berra

If the policy context in which schools work is changing in confusing and contradictory ways along the lines indicated in the previous chapter, then the world in which this policy is enacted, the world which our pupils inhabit, is also changing in significantly different ways.

It is not solely the responsibility of schools to prepare young people to understand and shape the increasingly complex future, but schools do have an important part to play. The accelerating pace of change, the expanding range of factors driving change, and the complexity of the interrelationships between specific changes, means that there is an ironic wisdom in the saying attributed to Yogi Berra. Preparing children (and even adults) for living in the future means acknowledging that the only certainty is constant change in almost every aspect of life.

Making predictions about the future is, in most cases, unreliable. Predictions are particularly unsafe if used to make detailed plans. However, the omnipresence of change, and its impact on every aspect of our lives, means that we have to pay more attention to, and increase our understanding of, future trends and develop more reliable forecasts. Ultimately, the aim is to be able to embrace and work with a fluid conception of the future which we constantly review and revise as part of our present.

Others have provided broad and detailed analyses of future global trends, particularly relating to specific factors, so our intention here is rather to focus upon a number of key changes which may have particular relevance for education and learning. We start by looking at ten significant global trends. It is also essential to relate these to the specific locality in which you live and work, as variations in context will affect both the relevance of different factors and their impact. We look at how the global impacts on the local in the second part of this chapter. At the end of each section we have suggested a few questions to stimulate your own reflections and discussions with colleagues. We also hope that you will form your own questions.

1. Life expectancy is increasing

People are living longer and life expectancy continues to increase. The statistical bulletin on the population of the UK, published by the Office for National Statistics (ONS) in June 2017, states that the 'UK population continues to age' (Office for National Statistics, 2017). This is consistent with population trends in all other developed countries. According to the same ONS bulletin, by mid-2016, the proportion of the UK population aged 65 and over had reached 18%, and whilst this represents a temporary slowing in the growth of the proportion of older people, the trend is expected to continue, with only immigration increasing the proportion of younger age groups significantly.

Sixty-year-olds today might expect to live for another 30 years, until they are 90. Figures from the ONS show that there were more than half a million people aged over 90 in the UK in 2014. This is 5% of the population, compared with 2% of the population 30 years previously (reported in Elliott, 2016). In *The 100-Year Life: Living and Working in an Age of Longevity*, Lynda Gratton and Andrew Scott (2016b) note that today's 20-year-olds might expect to live until they are 105.

The consequence of this is that the conception of life in three phases – childhood and education, followed by work, then retirement – is no longer valid (Gratton and Scott, 2016a). For our long lives to also be active and fulfilled, we will need to be adaptable. Effective, continuous learning will enable us to negotiate a range of life changes. Some writers are questioning the validity of the idea of retirement, suggesting instead that older age will be characterised by different types of economic activity and social contribution (see Mason, 2015: 284–286; Srnicek and Williams, 2015: 117–123).

Within developed countries, where the proportion of people in different age groups is becoming more equal, intergenerational relationships are changing and becoming more important. The Resolution Foundation has convened an Intergenerational Commission, bringing together leaders from business, academia, and policy-making, to explore issues of intergenerational fairness and to 'devise a means of repairing the social contract between generations' (Gardiner, 2016: 4). The establishment of the commission was motivated by a number of recent trends, most notably the likelihood that those born post-2000 will be the first generation to have lower lifetime earnings than previous generations, that levels of home ownership are significantly lower amongst younger people, and that the current distribution of the welfare state seems to benefit older generations (Gardiner, 2016: 5). A new or revised social contract between generations is becoming an issue that affects all aspects of people's lives – personal, social, political, and societal.

Questions for reflection and discussion

- How do we prepare children and young people to be lifelong learners?
- How do we engage, or re-engage, people with learning throughout all phases of life?
- How can education help to build intergenerational understanding and cohesion?

---

2. Global migration is going to continue

The population of the developed world is becoming more stable. The population of Europe in the twenty-first century is projected to fall from 742 million in 2017 to 653 million in 2100, whilst in North America it is projected to increase relatively slowly from 361 million in 2017 to 499 million in 2100. The population of Asia was 4,504 million in 2017; it is predicted to grow to 5,257 million by 2050, but then reduce to 4,780 million in 2100. The population of Africa is projected to continue to grow rapidly throughout the twenty-first century, from 1,256 million in 2017, to 2,528 million in 2050 and reaching 4,468 million by 2100 (United Nations, Department of Economic and Social Affairs, Population Division, 2017: 1).

The UN Population Division report states that the overall trend is for the rate of global population growth to slow, with future growth dependent upon changing fertility levels in different countries and across continents. Fertility levels are highest in Africa and Asia, although the projection is for rates of growth to slow in Asia in the second half of the twenty-first century. More than half of world population growth between now and 2050 is expected to occur in Africa, where an estimated 1.3 billion of the total 2.2 billion people will be added to the global population. Asia is projected to be the second largest contributor with 750 million more people (United Nations, Department of Economic and Social Affairs, Population Division, 2017: 3).

As fertility levels decline in a country, so the age distribution changes as fewer children are added, making the number of older people proportionally higher. Life expectancy is increasing globally and in all regions, with the greatest gains in Africa where life expectancy increased by 6.6 years between 2000–2005 and 2010–2015, compared with 3.6 years globally. In 2010–2015, life expectancy in Africa was 60.2 years compared with 71.8 in Asia, 74.6 in Latin America and the Caribbean, 77.2 years in Europe, and 77.9 years in Oceania and North America (United Nations, Department of Economic and Social Affairs, Population Division, 2017: 7).

In some regions, increased life expectancy is accompanied by falling birth rates, resulting in more of the population being in older age groups, but in many regions the populations are comparatively young. In Africa, children under the age of 15 account for 41% of the population and those aged 15 to 24 for an additional 19% (United Nations, Department of Economic and Social Affairs, Population Division, 2017: 10). The UN's 2030 Agenda for Sustainable Development highlights the importance of providing health care, education, and employment opportunities for these young people coming from the poorest countries and groups (United Nations, Department of Economic and Social Affairs, Population Division, 2017: 10).

The UN's 2030 Agenda for Sustainable Development draws attention to the international and regional migration that is occurring as a consequence of the demographic and socio-economic differences between regions. It recognises that 'international migration can be a positive force for economic and social development', which serves to 'increase the global productivity of labour' (United Nations, Department of Economic and Social Affairs, Population Division, 2017: 9). According to the UN's data, net migration increased steadily from 1950 to 2010, with Europe,

North America, and Oceania being net receivers and Africa, Asia, and Latin America net senders. From 2000 to 2010, the net inflow into Europe, North America, and Oceania reached 3.1 million per year, with some signs of decline in the subsequent five years. The key drivers of international migration are identified as 'large and persistent economic and demographic asymmetries', which are expected to continue, with the United States, Germany, Canada, the United Kingdom, Australia, and the Russian Federation projected to be the largest receivers (United Nations, Department of Economic and Social Affairs, Population Division, 2017: 10).

Another key driver of international and regional migration is local conflict and environmental disaster. These are much harder to predict but can have a significant impact upon the resources and communities of neighbouring regions when significant populations migrate to preserve their safety and well-being. The situation in the Eastern Mediterranean illustrates the difficulty of distinguishing between economic migrants and refugees.

Global events necessarily raise many moral and ethical questions. The nature of modern media means that children have awareness of world events from a very early age, without necessarily understanding the context of the images they are seeing. For example, how is a 5-year-old supposed to make sense of the images of families crammed into small boats arriving on beaches, crying with relief or at something much worse? Is it the job of schools to help them understand this?

Some children may experience an enhanced sense of connection and empathy through the heritage of relatives or school friends. However, other communities may experience a sense of threat or seek to blame migration for local difficulties – for example, pressures on employment opportunities, a lack of available housing, and declining public services, such as health and education. Many of these communities have been insulated against recent social changes and progress. Socially and culturally cohesive, they have often not benefited from the economic and industrial investment that they see in other areas. The decline of traditional industry and employment opportunities will only enhance such experiences. Global migration raises different educational questions in these contexts, which are equally important, but with different perspectives and aspirations to be considered.

The political decisions made by national governments (individually and collectively), and in local areas, could alter the effect of migration for periods of time, but are not going to substantially change the global movement of people. They are, however, likely to have a greater impact upon the attitudes of individuals and communities, informed by their experiences and perceptions. Arguably, in a globalised world, young people need to be prepared to network and to learn to collaborate regionally, nationally, and globally to extend their experiences and widen their perceptions. This requires an attitude and approach that is outward looking, eager to explore, to understand, and to empathise with global humanity. The insularity that accompanies negative attitudes towards migration will almost certainly inhibit horizons and aspirations. There is a risk that communities, including the young, will seek to hold onto and reinforce local, traditional characteristics, closing off from cultural and demographic change rather than debating how to maximise future potential for the community, individuals, and their families. Socio-cultural contexts are important in helping to define our sense of identity and who we are. They can also determine our outlook on the world and how far we are able and prepared to embrace diversity in our lives and relationships.

Questions for reflection and discussion

- When and how should schools begin to explore the moral and ethical questions raised by migration?
- How is migration impacting upon your locality and on people's likely future? How can this be discussed with families and communities?
- How should children and young people be developed into 'global citizens'?

---

3. The environment is changing

The total number of people and proportion of the population living in urban areas are growing rapidly. By 2050, the United Nations (2014: xxi) estimates that 66% of the world's population will live in urban areas. This trend applies in England and the rest of the UK, with an increasing proportion of the population living in London and the South East. On average, people travel further each day to work and to access essential services, spending more time in a car or on public transport. The analysis by the ONS shows that the average distance commuted to work increased from 13.4 km in 2001 to 15 km in 2011, with full-time, male workers travelling furthest and longer journeys more likely to be made by rail (Office for National Statistics, 2014). For many, it is the norm for everyday tasks to involve a car journey rather than a walk.

Population density and traffic congestion impacts upon air quality and the wider environment, affecting some regions and localities more than others. The impact of climate change continues to affect every region of the world, with developed countries not immune. The world is continuing to become warmer year by year.[1] Extreme weather events and climate disruption cause infrastructure damage, threaten continued habitation in some areas, and make sustainable agriculture more difficult, including in parts of the UK. One immediate effect of this disruption is increased migration within countries and across continents.

Essential resources are diminishing. The rate of use of mineral resources in recent years has accelerated as developing countries aim to catch up economically and industrially with the developed world. In many areas throughout the world water is increasingly insufficient to meet growing demands, a trend further exacerbated by climate change. The transition to environmentally

---

1   The Union of Concerned Scientists state that every one of the past 40 years has been warmer than the twentieth-century average; that 2016 was the hottest year on record; and that the 12 warmest years on record have all occurred since 1998. See http://www.ucsusa.org/global_warming#.WZMMXa2ZO1s.

sustainable technologies is slower than the growth in global demand. Very few of us voluntarily limit our personal lifestyle to help conserve the environment, other than in superficial ways.

In the UK, recent austerity policies have resulted in reduced spending on parks and recreational facilities, and many have been privatised. In some localities, other apparently public spaces (for instance, Canary Wharf and Bishops Square in Spitalfields, London) have been privatised, in some instances restricting access to the more wealthy (Shenker, 2017). Other factors can contribute to unequal access to the countryside and natural environment, including limited available transport and its cost, the pressures of work, and changing working patterns.

Environmental changes have implications for almost every aspect of the lives of people throughout the world. The global trend is towards more people experiencing urban living, increased congestion, squeezed public services, more time spent travelling, and fewer opportunities to relax and enjoy the great outdoors. Frequently having the opportunity to enjoy and develop an understanding of the natural world is arguably essential to well-being and spirituality, and is a basis for learning throughout life.

Questions for reflection and discussion

- What role can the regular experience of the natural world play in developing happy, healthy, and safe children and young people?
- What role does environmental education play in promoting citizenship?
- What are the personal choices that everyone can make about their own lives and lifestyles that can contribute to improving the environment and our experience of the world?

---

4. We live and learn in a virtual world

The pace and scale of technological change means that it is hard to predict with any accuracy what new developments will become part of our everyday existence within the next five years, let alone the next 10 or 20 years. Changes in technology will potentially have a massive effect on our lives, and will likely raise moral issues and risks. Children and young people will need to be equipped to deal with an uncertain technological future. For example, new developments can merge the digital and physical worlds so that we can enter augmented landscapes and experience relationships with augmented 'people' in a new virtual reality. This virtual world can appear as real as reality. For a child growing up in a world in which virtual reality is the norm, how they will distinguish the virtual from the 'real' world?

The potential learning benefits of communication technology are immense. A simple internet search means that information on a topic is immediately available. We can also find limitless guidance on how to do things; explanations of how things work; interpretations of ideas and concepts; opinions about events; and ideologies, propaganda, and polemics. In an internet age, judgement and the ability to discriminate between sources becomes even more crucial. It also means that learning can take place anywhere, anytime, and with anyone anywhere in the world – no longer constrained by the requirements of institutions. There is thus the potential for anyone with access to information technology and the internet to personalise learning and to choose their (virtual) teacher. But, again, sound judgement is called for.

Questions for reflection and discussion

- What role will educational organisations and professionals play in the world of technological communication in the future?
- What are the basic skills of lifelong learning for the future?
- What does critical thinking look like in the virtual world?
- How can opportunities for greater personalisation of learning be organised to ensure greatest benefit for all?
- How can people access support and guidance for their learning throughout their lives?

5. Friendships, families, and relationships are becoming more flexible and varied: both on and offline

We have become used to the constant connectivity that personal technology and social media has brought to our lives. It is not uncommon for people to never really switch off from their devices – both in terms of keeping up with their online social networks and maintaining an awareness of world events. This opens up possibilities for new relationships and networks that can rapidly change and become increasingly complex. It also raises issues of personal privacy and identity as our devices provide details of where we are and with whom, as well as with whom we may be communicating and when.

Whilst in the past, childhood friends were most likely peers from school or from the neighbourhood, it is now common for young people to have vast and varied online networks. We are also seeing a shift when it comes to family relationships, with the traditional nuclear family becoming less common. It is now routine for people to have several significant relationships during the course of their lives, with the consequence of fragmented and interrelated families. Family relationships and close personal friendships can be expected to change and have varying degrees of significance over time. Negotiating such changes in significant relationships will be important for the emotional health and well-being both of the individuals concerned and the network of people around them. Some children may experience family break up early in their lives, but for others this may occur much later or not at all.

In the global, connected world of today the ability to develop social relationships with a wide range of people has never been so important. This includes direct social contact and the ability to network using social media. Evidence suggests that inequalities in social capital are increasing, and that even those who have achieved educational success can find themselves disadvantaged when competing with peers whose family and wider social networks can provide financial support or open doors to career opportunities which are shut to open competition (Social Mobility Commission, 2017: 77–78). Social relationships and networking skills can increase social capital for the community, thus raising aspirations and success. Communities that are rich in social capital have organisations that provide opportunities and experiences that are wider than those of families and friendship groups. Traditionally these were often found in organisations such as churches and religious bodies, trade unions and work-related societies, sports clubs, and cultural groups. As society has become more individualistic, many of these have declined and become less influential, particularly in socially deprived areas, where greater limits on people's personal incomes and time mean they are less able to sustain them.

The power and reach of global technological companies, such as Facebook and Google, is such that they collect and store vast quantities of data about the majority of individuals in most countries. As a result, they hold more data about our friendships, profile, interests, hobbies, and habits than governments and other public bodies, and this volume is increasing. They also use the information to make money by selling our profile data to companies and even political parties (see Booth and Mason, 2017; Cadwalladr, 2017; Lewis, 2017). The large-scale release of this 'secure', secret, and personal data has implications that we might consider to be beneficial in some circumstances – for example, when it increases our knowledge of governments, businesses, or organisations – but could also be dangerous for our own personal privacy. As users of social media and communication technology, everyone needs to be aware of the many risks that are ever-present in everything we do, including the threat of financial fraudsters, identity theft, bullies, trolls, and those who seek to gain trust to exploit vulnerabilities. Furthermore, the sharing of personal photographs and experiences online could have long-term implications for future relationships and opportunities in the real world.

Questions for reflection and discussion

- What are the elements of safe and secure use of communication technology? How can these be developed from an early age in preparation for lifelong use?

- What interpersonal skills do children and young people need to develop for the varied social contexts they are likely to encounter?

- How is learning being affected by the varied circumstances in which children live?

- How can children be supported to establish an extensive multimedia social network that safely and effectively promotes their abilities, talents, personality, and interests?

---

6. Economic activity is increasingly less likely to be defined as employment

The nature of work has been changing continuously for many decades, and will continue to change. Some shifts have come because of technological advances, whilst others are a result of changes to the structure of the economy or because of legislation. These changes will not only persist but are likely to accelerate, to the extent that the traditional distinction between work and leisure no longer hold. In the future, it is increasingly likely that people will have more time available to decide what to do, at least at certain points in their lives. Such ideas have for many years appeared to be a futuristic fantasy, but current trends in life expectancy and the impact of technology on future employment suggest that this is the direction in which we are moving.

Technological developments are gradually automating activity that has long been regarded as dependent on people. Driverless vehicles are currently being tested and many new cars offer driverless features, such as automated parking. Driverless transport is being developed by many companies throughout the world, with some aspects already incorporated into family cars produced by a number of manufacturers. Once automated vehicles become widespread, there is the potential for significant consequences for those who earn a living from driving.

Other unmanned systems are continuing to replace people in the workplace, including in employment sectors previously considered to be safe. For example, software that can listen to and answer questions is being developed with the enhanced capacity to learn from experience. If this could be fully utilised, employment in many white-collar areas such as retail, call centres, and aspects of legal and administrative work will likely diminish. Technology could liberate people from repetitive jobs or have profound social consequences resulting from increased unemployment: this will depend partly on political choices and policy, but also on how people respond.

In the last three decades, there have been growing economic inequalities, globally and within the UK. The differences between the wealth, health, and lifestyle of the 'global elite' and 'the rest' are increasing continuously. Evidence suggests that social mobility is diminishing, with those who have least being least able to improve their life chances (Social Mobility Commission, 2017: 4).

The nature and structure of employment is also changing, and not only for those with limited education and low skill levels. Currently there are contradictory trends. Employment for many is less than secure. Zero hours contracts and freelance or portfolio working can all mean uncertain hours from week to week, resulting in some people needing to hold a sequence of jobs, with income coming from several sources. For the low paid, this can mean juggling a number of part-time jobs in order to provide earnings that are barely sufficient. For others, job insecurity can mean periods of unemployment, which in the worst cases are structural. Many people can no longer expect to have a career and 'a job for life'. Nor can they expect to have a linear series of jobs. An increasing number of families, especially those on low incomes, are dependent on having several sources of income at any one time, and have to change continuously to adapt to circumstance.

A growing number of people work longer hours for less. Research published by the Trades Union Congress (TUC, 2015) shows that since 2010 the number of people working excessive hours (defined as more than 48 hours per week) has increased by 15%. In the UK, more than five million people worked an average of 7.7 hours a week unpaid overtime in 2016 (TUC, 2017). This is despite some research predicting a loss of jobs in many sectors because of automation. Evidence as to whether changes in the labour market will mean fewer jobs is inconclusive, but changes in employment are increasingly valuing people with technological skills, with other lower level skills being replaced by automation (UK Commission for Employment and Skills, 2014: 4–6).

Perhaps the way in which schools talk about preparing learners for employment is already outmoded. It is arguable that we require a new language for economic activity that no longer refers to the 'world of work', 'careers advice', and 'preparing for jobs' but recognises that how people earn their income will constantly vary and may have several different and changing aspects. In such circumstances, some of the qualities required will be economic resilience (i.e. the ability to recover from and adjust to negative impacts of external economic shocks – for example, loss of employment and income), networking skills, adaptability, skill transference, rapid learning, and creativity.

We should also begin to question the meaning and purpose of economic activity, and to consider what would give us personal satisfaction and allow us to contribute to society in ways that are not just economic. Work should not be associated purely with drudgery, and assessments of worth should not be made in exclusively economic terms. In *Inventing the Future*, Nick Srnicek and Alex Williams (2015) argue that we should start planning for a world in which we work less and they explore what this might be like. One suggestion, which is actually being given serious consideration by some politicians, is for the social security system to be dramatically overhauled so that all citizens receive a basic income as a right (e.g. Brooks, 2017). Engagement in further economic activity would open up more possibilities for choice.

Whatever the future might bring, it seems highly likely that people will have far more choice about how they use their time and engage economically. If our basic earning capacity were secure, we could instead focus on the sense of self-worth, personal satisfaction, and value we can derive from what we choose to do.

Questions for reflection and discussion

- In preparing young people for the future, how do we prepare them to make choices about what to do and why?
- What are the implications for aspirations if the question 'What are you going to do in your life?' is not defined entirely by the job you do?
- Do we require a fundamental rethink of the way we talk about economic activity and how we conceive of using our time?

---

7. Well-being, lifestyle, and life expectancy are interrelated factors

Whilst on average life expectancy is increasing, there are marked differences based on social class, occupation, and geographical region (see Office for National Statistics, 2015). Advances in health care mean that many people live longer, despite having medical conditions that in the past would have resulted in an earlier death. However, length of life also has to be considered in relation to quality of life, as debates about assisted dying have highlighted. Should we keep someone alive simply because we can if their quality of life is such that this may not be in their best interest or what they want?

There is a growing understanding of how diet and lifestyle in early life can have a significant impact upon our health and well-being throughout the rest of our life. Whilst we can have genetic predispositions towards particular medical conditions and whilst we will have inherited many of our physical attributes, what we eat, the exercise we take, and other choices we make about substance use – such as whether we drink alcohol or take drugs – affect our health, quality of life, and life expectancy. Put simply, the lifestyle choices we make will affect the life we have now and in the future.

Smartphone apps and fitness trackers can now provide a constant report on our physical health and well-being. For some, the information provided might help to improve fitness and overall health by prompting individuals to take more control of their personal health and well-being. The initial focus of these apps was originally to help individuals monitor their physical activity and personal fitness, diet, and weight. More recent developments have extended the range of uses into medicine, to monitor specific aspects of health, such as heart rate, blood pressure, and blood sugar levels. For some, this technology helps them to manage their medication and monitor their condition, providing alerts to enable further medical intervention when necessary. This can give individuals more independence, make treatments more effective, and reduce costs for medical services as people become increasingly able to manage their conditions effectively.

Understanding of how the brain develops and functions is increasing rapidly and this has the potential to improve learning and attainment. The development of biotech drugs, which could enhance brain functioning and performance in healthy children, raises ethical concerns for school leaders, parents, and wider society. One survey by *Nature* magazine found that 'one-third of respondents said they would feel pressure to give cognition-enhancing drugs to their children if other children at school were taking them' (Maher, 2008).

For many years schools have encouraged healthy eating and provided food at different times throughout the day in an effort to improve learning. Attention has again been given to the role that daily exercise can play in improving well-being and performance in the classroom (see Ridley, 2017).[2] In the future, technology may offer the potential to monitor students' health and well-being using a range of different measures and to intervene in different ways, which will, arguably, have beneficial lifelong implications.

The evidence is that the eating habits and patterns of behaviour we establish in early life become embedded and stay with us throughout our lives (NHS Choices, 2016). Early years and primary education, therefore, have an important role to play in developing families' and children's understanding of how to manage their diet, fitness, and lifestyle choices to establish habits that provide for long-term health and happiness. Similarly, education and learning programmes throughout adolescence and adult life should arguably incorporate elements that reinforce healthy lifestyles to boost attainment and satisfaction.

Questions for reflection and discussion

- How should schools make use of neuroscientific understanding of how learning can be improved?
- How can schools work with families and communities to promote healthy lifestyles in order to improve current and future performance and attainment?
- How should schools make their values in relation to health and well-being explicit, as part of their wider values and ethos?
- Should dimensions of students' well-being be monitored and assessed as part of an assessment of performance?

---

2 See also http://thedailymile.co.uk/.

8. Identities are formed not given

For most of us, our identity is largely established by the factors and circumstances of our births. At birth, aspects of our gender and race are prescribed genetically, but then aspects of our identity are largely culturally developed. Included within this, to a very large extent, would be our sexuality, ethnicity, religion, educational opportunities, future occupation, where and how we chose to live, and life chances. From a very early age, children are socialised into an awareness of what is expected of them and what they can expect. If they make choices that go against these expectations, then they may be ostracised socially and potentially disowned by their families. Becoming a member of a different religion, marrying someone of a different ethnicity or faith, or even moving to another region might be unwelcome in a particular community, and so is for many unobtainable (even if desirable).

Whilst social pressures continue, and are greater in some communities than others, the complexity, flexibility, and mobility offered by access to different social networks and groupings means that most of us have the opportunity to decide and create our own identity or identities. Even aspects of identity considered as biologically determined, such as gender and race, are now being claimed as a matter of personal choice. In general, and particularly within western, developed societies and cultures, there is increased tolerance of diversity and the prevailing social attitude is that the individual is free to choose who they are and how they wish to live.

People construct complex identities that have different facets in different parts of their lives. How each individual constructs and defines their identity is becoming an increasingly important question. A multiple identity, with a number of different elements that have tensions or conflicts between them, can be problematic and can affect general mental health and well-being. In the future, it is likely that we all will construct our own personal *hybrid* identity, within which it will be important to ensure that there is a clarity and sense of who we are, what we value, and how we wish to present ourselves to others.

How we are able to define our identity is a prerequisite of being comfortable in our own skin. In the future, how each individual develops their own identity will be critical for their happiness, well-being, and success throughout life. This recognition has important developmental and educational implications in at least two respects:

1   The provision of personal support and mentoring to individuals, required in different contexts and throughout life.

2   Providing approaches to support and enable children and young people to develop *personal agency* in building their sense of self and identity as a basis for being a strong, confident, creative, and resilient person in all aspects of their life.

Questions for reflection and discussion

- How do schools empower and develop personal agency in everyone?
- How are children and young people mentored to develop their sense of self and confidence in their own identities?
- How do schools work with communities to support and respect the rights of individuals?
- How do schools develop collaborative and team working that respects and welcomes differences in personal identities?

9. The meaning and nature of democracy is changing and becoming less certain

The established political order appears much less certain than it once did, with parties on the far ends of the spectrum upsetting the usual broadly centrist order in many western countries. Elections in many countries in Europe, and in the United States, have shown that many voters are disillusioned with the centre-right and centre-left parties that have traditionally been dominant. Support for parties of the far right and left, nationalist parties, and parties that advocate independence for particular regions has grown. Such voting patterns reflect differences within societies, with increased risk of segregation and community tensions, which can in turn be open to being exploited by extremist or terrorist groups. Increased nationalism has been interpreted as a response to the consequences of globalisation. Some communities feel 'left behind' and perceive that they are not being sufficiently protected from economic disadvantage, whether because jobs are being exported overseas or because immigrants are 'taking their jobs': a perception that can be fuelled and fed upon by political parties for their own gains. For many, politicians appear part of a remote governing elite, detached and divorced from the communities that have elected them, furthering disengagement with traditional politics.

Voting patterns for several decades indicate that the age profile of those who vote is becoming increasingly skewed to older people, with many young people not voting. Consequently, political parties promote policies that favour the elderly, whilst other policies, such as raising tuition fees, will have long-term consequences for younger people. One possible outcome will be to further disillusion young people with the current political system, although there are some indications in the UK and other countries that it is the engagement of young people in politics that is challenging the established party machines and hence the status quo (Curtis, 2017).

Alongside these trends, the nature of political engagement is changing with the use of social media. It could be argued that young people are more likely to engage with specific issues through social media rather than through traditional parties at election time. Reduced support for mainstream parties has been interpreted as a consequence of an increase in engagement in specific issues through social media and other campaigns (Bartlett et al., 2011). Such campaigns also appear to be having an increasing influence on governments and party policies, which means that people can feel that they are able to exercise more influence than they would by casting a vote for a party that appears to be very like its opponents.

However, it is also possible that the results of elections are being influenced by how social media can be used by powerful political forces covertly and in ways that are very difficult to monitor and regulate. The 2016 presidential election in the United States saw allegations that Russia hacked the emails of, in particular, leading members of the Democratic Party and used these to spread misinformation. Some have suggested the results of both the US presidential election and the EU referendum in the UK may have been influenced by the use of psychometric profiles to target groups of voters on social media sites like Facebook (e.g. Doward and Gibbs, 2017).

How these trends might result in changes in our democratic systems and structures in the future is unclear. In England, current policies at the time of writing are reducing the power and responsibilities of local government with a move to establishing regional mayors, but it is unclear how these might develop across the country as a whole. The Brexit referendum result has also raised many questions about the UK's democratic structures which are likely to take years to fully resolve. The mainstream media are being questioned and challenged, as is as the role of an independent judiciary to interpret the law. All of this reflects the growing complexity of the world today and the way in which the attitudes and views of many people can be easily manipulated by misinformation, slogans, and simplistic narratives by those with extreme ideologies.

All these trends raise questions about the nature of citizenship in the future and how children and young people should be educated to play an active role in democratic systems in their own country and to engage with contemporary global issues. Political agency that is limited to supporting social media campaigns is unlikely to provide a sense of fulfilment to those who want to make a difference in the long term. Remote governments and global companies, with apparently limitless power, are also likely to contribute to an increased sense of disillusionment and powerlessness amongst young people, whilst populist governments elected by playing on the fears and sense of injustice of certain groups of voters are likely to aggravate tensions and increase divisions within and between countries.

The consequences of these trends are uncertain. They raise questions about the future of democratic systems both in the UK and throughout the world: questions that may fall to future generations to answer. It would seem impossible to reduce global conflict without maintaining stable democratic systems, in which citizens participate in an informed and meaningful way.

Questions for reflection and discussion

- How can young people be given experience of political agency from an early age?
- How should schools contribute to and sometimes lead local political debate and action?
- How do we define 'political engagement' in the world of social media and in a 'global village'?

---

10. The world is becoming increasingly dangerous

A report published by the Ministry of Defence (2014) considers how our world is likely to change by 2045. The report identifies threats, challenges, and defence and security implications under 13 broad thematic areas, with the overall impression that the world is becoming less safe, and that this will impact upon all countries and societies to a greater or lesser extent. Some of the main trends identified include:

- The potential for growing numbers of conflicts globally over scarce resources, most particularly water.
- Population growth and increasing numbers living in urban areas, which without adequate infrastructure could result in risks of communicable diseases and poverty leading to 'violent insurgencies'.
- Continuing growth in the power and influence of multinationals, with some 'providing services that used to be the responsibility of the state', including security forces.
- Increasing threats from terrorists and criminals with access to advanced technology (e.g. cyber-attacks, drones, environmental warfare) (Ministry of Defence, 2014: xiii–xiv).

The complexity of the modern world can be both daunting and confusing for children and young people, especially if they have a questioning mind and are motivated to make a difference in situations they find unacceptable or morally corrupt. Ideologies which offer a single, clear narrative to explain the world, and how to change it, can be very seductive, and the internet provides a means to spread these ideas and messages quickly.

The continuing globalisation of extremist ideologies and terrorism and the destabilisation of cohesion in communities are interrelated and demonstrate how global events have local impact and how local events can become global. In an interconnected world, nowhere can be immune from global issues. Consequently, the response of countries, regions, and communities will contribute to, and impact on, everyone's lives. Our individual understanding of, and response to, the complex interplay of factors will in itself impact on our sense of safety and security. A rise in nationalist, populist parties in western democracies could also have consequences for international relations and ideological narratives. If leading western countries become more insular, inward-looking, and seemingly self-interested, this could destabilise the international bodies that we have historically relied upon to respond to global crises and seek to resolve conflicts.

Many extremist ideologies seek to challenge democracy and overthrow democratic systems. For some young people, these extreme ideologies and ideas can be seductive and, when this is coupled with broad political disengagement, it should no longer be taken for granted that all young people will perceive the benefits of democracy or regard it as the best political model.

Technology is now very accessible and consumer demand for the latest technologies exists throughout the world. New technological developments are not inherently good or bad. Ultimately, whether they prove to be beneficial or detrimental to individuals or societies will depend upon how we use them, and for what purpose. Widespread availability and proliferation of new technologies is arguably resulting in increased risks to personal safety and security. We cannot foresee exactly how technology will develop in the future, or how people will use it. For example, as technology has become increasingly sophisticated, so has cybercrime. The pace of innovation means this raises ethical questions, without the opportunity for detailed consideration and public debate. Increased opportunities for personal agency are accompanied by increased personal and social responsibilities – for example, respecting privacy and not hiding behind anonymity to be threatening and abusive. Education for the future involves preparing young people – as well as adults, communities, and societies – to respond to the unknowns of tomorrow, not just offering direction and guidance based upon what is happening now.

Questions for reflection and discussion

- How do we prepare children to be at ease with complexity and to recognise the dangers of simplistic slogans and distorted ideologies?
- How can young people learn to recognise the early signs of tension and separation that can lead to conflict, violence, and the breakdown of social safety and order?
- What role does everyday language play in our attitudes towards and treatment of others, particularly those who are different from us in how they live and what they believe?
- How do our personal values and worldviews affect our role as school leaders?
- What role can schools play within communities in promoting cohesion and a local interpretation and understanding of global issues?

The global is the local

One of the dominant features of the complex and interrelated world of today is how interconnectivity has effectively made the world smaller. What happens in one place can have an almost instantaneous impact in other localities as news about world events proliferates at the click of a button. In outlining the complexity of global trends in the twenty-first century, we have repeatedly highlighted the interrelationship between global and local factors.

In some ways, it can appear that the world is becoming more homogenous with instant communication linking disparate people and places, and multinationals having a presence in even the most remote and unlikely places. However, it is essential not to lose sight of the particular characteristics of local contexts and how these influence the views, attitudes, and aspirations of local communities. For example, in June 2016 the referendum on the UK's membership of the European Union demonstrated people's difference of views on the future of the country and its place in the world. Most commentators agree, regardless of their own views on the issue, that the result was influenced by many people feeling that politicians and the establishment were ignoring their views and interests, potentially indicating a wider dissatisfaction with democratic processes. The voting patterns also indicated generational and regional differences, with some areas reportedly feeling excluded from the prosperity enjoyed by London and the South East of England (Electoral Commission, 2016; Moore, 2016).

One of the characteristics of the interconnected world is how the global becomes the local and the local can become global. One of the major challenges then, lies in analysing and understanding exactly how the two are interrelated and interconnected. The hierarchical, top-down model that has been dominant for much of history seems increasingly not to provide sustainable ways forward for the future. We need to reconceptualise to recognise that interconnections happen globally, without the traditional barriers of education, class, ethnicity, or status.

In educational terms, as we have argued in Chapter 1, learning requires rethinking and redesigning in a number of ways. One of the key principles is to recognise that a 'one size fits all' approach is outmoded. Just as the learning needs of each child are different, each school, and each local context, is unique. It becomes the responsibility of those who live and work in each context to apply their local knowledge and understanding to identify how global changes might impact locally and vice versa. Equally, school leaders need to develop a knowledge and understanding of local changes to inform how they prepare children and young people for the future. This will be best achieved through an engagement with local communities and with young people themselves, as they will contribute to the creation of the future.

To reiterate the point from a different perspective, the schools that do effectively prepare children for the future will increasingly be those schools that are an active part of the communities to which students belong. Whilst there will be a common core to the curriculum and its content, the design and pedagogy used for effective delivery should be varied to fit the locality. Engaging students in their learning also requires an understanding of the issues that concern them and the questions they are asking about the world in which they are growing up.

The local context, therefore, needs to be built into the design and delivery of the curriculum, and reflected in the culture and ethos of schools, as they engage with communities to raise aspirations and achievement and help construct a new future. So, what factors do we need to explore in order to develop a deeper understanding and which are likely to have an impact on outcomes?

Key factors affecting local change trends

In developing a shared understanding with communities and other key partners, and an increased knowledge of change within the locality, we need to consider several key factors. What follows is intended as a starting point to stimulate discussion in your school and with community partners. Our experience is that once schools engage in this process, they develop new understanding of and insights into their communities, and what the community thinks to be important and influential. It is to be expected that any factor that has a significant impact on one community could affect another in an entirely different way, or not at all.

Demographics

There are very few regions in which the demographic profile is not changing. It will be important to understand what the changes are, why they are occurring, and what the impact will be in the next 10, 20, or 30 years.

Demographic factors to explore locally could include:

- Population variations related to age, ethnicity and socio-economic status.
- Migration both into and out of the area.
- Variations in the ethnicities and faiths of the local population.
- The stability of the population – the proportion of people who have lived in the area for a long period compared with those who have come to the area recently, either transiently or to settle.
- Whether current changes reflect long-term patterns, or are short-term and caused by particular circumstances.
- Population projections for the area for the future.

This is made more difficult by the fact that accurate, up-to-date data is difficult to obtain in some areas, particularly where demographic changes are dynamic. The collection of official statistics often struggles to keep pace with changes and mobility within local areas. Often in these contexts, schools and health services can have more accurate records than those available to local authorities and policy-makers.

Some pupils will come to school having experienced profound trauma, displacement, or uncertainty. Arguably, the immediate challenge for school leaders in these circumstances lies in determining how to meet the needs of these children now. However, the questions this raises about the education provided by the school now and in future are not separate. A school's ethos, curriculum, and provision must aim to make sense of complex and interrelated contextual factors, both now and in the future.

Employment and economic activity

Employment opportunities vary significantly in different areas – compare rural and urban; large cities and smaller towns; coast and inland; north and south. Changes to traditional industries continue to impact more on some communities, with the greatest effect occurring in areas which have previously had one significant source of employment with limited diversity. If a large proportion of the adults in a community work in the local factory, consider the effects its closure would have. In some areas, this void of employment opportunities is never adequately filled. Some areas will have a wealth of opportunities and transport links that facilitate choice. Others may have many more applicants than job vacancies.

There seems to also be a shift in the terms of employment that people can expect, with increasing numbers of people classified as self-employed (in some cases dubiously) or reliant on income from a number of different jobs, often with insecure hours and changing expectations. Growing numbers of people are also working from home for at least some of the time, as larger employers, including some local authorities and public services, seek to reduce office accommodation. Such changes will affect family life in different ways and influence the degree to which families can spend time together, share in and support activities, and supervise private study and learning together at home.

Employment and economic factors to explore locally could include:

- The types of work done by parents and carers.
- Any gender, ethnic, or socio-economic differences in employment patterns within the area and influences on attitudes and aspirations.
- The hours that parents and carers work and how regular these are.
- Involvement of other family members or social networks in providing childcare due to work commitments.
- Changes in the locality that could affect employment opportunities.
- The types of education and skills needed for work and how secure and transferable these are in the medium to long term.
- Any significant differences in employment patterns between the older and younger generations.
- The impact of employment patterns on home life and family relationships.

Social and community cohesion

A range of factors can affect community cohesiveness, levels of which can change significantly in a short period of time. Change may occur as a result of particular influences – for example, new groups moving into an area or significant changes in employment prospects, like the closure of a local business – or in response to a specific event – for example, an accident or act of violence which polarises different parts of the community. Changes in levels of cohesiveness can be slow and creeping or can occur suddenly. In some cases, the impact on cohesiveness can appear to be greatest in areas which have been demographically stable for a long period of time and then experience relatively sudden changes in population – for example, when an area with a high proportion of older people living in owner-occupied homes witness an influx of younger families into privately rented accommodation.

Local authorities and police authorities have previously collected data that aimed to assess levels of community cohesiveness, but were no longer required to do this after the election of the coalition government in 2010, who built their strategy around the idea of integration. The data collected drew on a range of measures, including the views of local residents, levels of social mobility, employment rates, educational attainment, racial incidents, and crime statistics, including reported crime.[3] Meanwhile, for schools the statutory duty to promote community cohesion remains, but the coalition government removed the requirement for it to be evaluated as part of Ofsted inspections, removing accountability and effectively devaluing its importance. This is, therefore, a good example of how changes in government can change national policy, and how essential it is for schools to determine their own priorities, in keeping with their values and principles.

Opportunities for people to mix together in public spaces can have a major influence on community cohesiveness. Poor town planning can result in more people using cars even for short local journeys, limiting the opportunities for the spontaneous interactions you might have whilst walking. Everyone will have some experience of how the levels of traffic and use of roads can affect the number of social interactions between neighbours and people in general. Similarly, parks and other outdoor public spaces provide opportunities for people to come together, if seen as safe and welcoming. A lack of such spaces within a locality will reduce the opportunities for communities to come together, with consequences for cohesiveness.

It is important not to regard community cohesiveness as purely relating to race and ethnicity, as sometimes defined. Social differences can also have consequences for how people within communities regard each other and interact, and this can often be more complex than it may appear on the surface. One head teacher of a school with a mainly white British intake identified a difference between families he described as 'working poor' and those who were living in poverty

---

3   A 2007 report from the Community Cohesion Group of Manchester City Council provides an example of how one local authority responded to the requirement to monitor community cohesion. See http://www.manchester.gov.uk/download/downloads/id/18018/community_cohesion_steering_group_report_2007. The National Policing Improvement Agency's *Cohesion Guide* also provides a good example of how authorities approach this duty. See http://library.college.police.uk/docs/npia/CohesionGuide.pdf.

and dependent upon benefits. Whilst living on the same estates and appearing to be very similar, children from these families demonstrated differences in values, attitudes, and aspirations within school. These were also recognised by family members, and occasionally surfaced as tensions within the community.

Cohesiveness is influenced by a number of factors. The lessons of history show that it can be fragile, and differences and social prejudices easily surface in response to particular events and stimuli. The risk of tensions arising, potentially leading to conflict, are greatest when degrees of integration between different groups are low and there are some aspects of separation and even segregation. The perception that particular demographic groups are a drain on local resources or are the cause of specific problems in the community can be exploited for political self-interest and to increase separation between communities. National and international events can also have an effect on communities. In the UK, for example, reported levels of hate crime against Polish migrants increased following the vote to leave the European Union (Agerholm, 2016). Another example is the experience of schools and colleges with students from both Jewish and Muslim communities which have encountered increased tensions when there are hostilities between Palestine and Israel. However, we have also encountered positive examples of communities coming together through events such as carnivals and festivals, with the potential for a positive legacy.

Factors to explore locally could include:

- The different community groups that can be identified and their distinctive features.
- Public spaces within the locality for the community to meet and mix together.
- Levels of integration demonstrated in housing, use of local facilities, religious practice, employment, leisure activities, and use of public services (schools, doctors, dentists).
- Commonly expressed attitudes about other communities or ethnic groups.
- Tensions between communities that could be triggered by events.
- The attitudes and aspirations towards education and schools that affect learning and relations between communities, students, family members, and the school.
- Contact with other public services and community groups regarding social and community cohesiveness.

Faith, religion, and beliefs

It can be easy to underestimate the continuing importance of religion in communities given the data showing falling attendance in Christian churches and the dominant secular nature of our society (Faith Survey, 2016). For faith schools, as well as other schools, there is the question of how open and aware they are of other faiths in the area and whether they allow for a questioning of pupils' own faith as an aspect of developing critical thinking. Belief systems shape our worldviews and, as such, could be said to have an influence on learning, and so are of relevance for schools. There is also the question of what people who do not identify with a particular faith or religious practice believe, even if this is not structured into an organised system. For example, do they believe in life after death, ghosts, a god or spirits, a supernatural power, a creator of the world, or nothing at all? How can schools offer a safe space for children to explore their own beliefs and those of others?

To understand the influence of faith and beliefs on learning, it is important to understand the influence particular faith groups have in communities. Faiths and religions can play a significant part in the culture of communities, both positively and negatively. Spirituality is an integral aspect of human life and part of our overall well-being. Given this, it is essential that school leaders have a good understanding of faith and beliefs in their local context and relate this to the ethos and culture of the school. This also needs to be reflected in their communication and partnerships with faith groups. It may be that the most important dialogue will be between those who hold different views.

Factors to explore locally could include:

- The places of worship, who leads them, and who attends.
- Places of worship outside of the immediate area that members of communities may travel to.
- More informal places of worship, such as houses or local meeting places, who organises gatherings, and who attends.
- Which pupils attend acts of worship or religious study regularly, and for which faiths.
- The teachings or belief systems of different faiths.
- Whether there are any aspects of belief which may have an impact on the learning or attitudes of students – for example, the view that learning takes place through instruction that resists questioning and self-directed learning; creationist beliefs; attitudes towards gender and sexuality that oppose certain subjects being taught and regard homosexuality as sinful; opposition to music and performance arts.

Social capital

In the Introduction to Part One, we gave the example of Roseto, Pennsylvania, and how a close-knit Italian-American community was formed from a disorganised, disparate group of Italian immigrants. Roseto is notable today because heart disease is much less prevalent than in similar, neighbouring communities. Wolf and Bruhn (1993: vii) concluded that a cohesive community had improved health and welfare; when a community demonstrates a lack of regard for others there is an opposite effect. Essentially, Roseto invested in building social capital and the benefits of that remained evident over time in the health and well-being of its citizens.

If we consider briefly the social capital of many communities in the UK, and the United States (Putnam, 2000), the picture appears to be one of decline. Many social institutions have disappeared or do not have the influence that they used to. Many churches and chapels have closed or are sustained by small, ageing congregations. The traditional industries that remain employ just a small proportion of the numbers they did in the past. Trade union membership has fallen, and social clubs and other community-based facilities are used regularly by much smaller numbers, who again are often elderly. Libraries and other public facilities are being shut, and local shopping centres lack the social vibrancy of the past, with fewer independent retailers and businesses.

In summary, the shift to individualism and consumerism has eroded the traditional social capital infrastructure of the past and, in many white British communities, it has been replaced by new organisations and facilities in only limited ways. This is often not the case in migrant communities who frequently work together and support each other, establishing new support networks. For many young people today, looking to make a start in employment, their aspirations can be limited by the relatives, friends, and networks of their parents. This reinforces the increasing inequalities within society, with some communities not possessing sufficient social capital to promote well-being and success.

Social capital is an important component of local culture and attitudes, and its strength can vary significantly between different areas and is increasingly affected by socio-economic factors. Schools, education, and learning are affected by this, which in turn means it is important for school leaders to understand local influences and potential.

Factors to explore locally could include:

- The social capital of local communities, who benefits and in what ways.
- Local organisations that contribute to social capital and the ways in which they do this.
- The ways in which the social capital of the local context helps to promote learning and educational outcomes.
- The potential for the school to stimulate and build social capital and collaborative community partnerships.

Interpreting these trends and the implications for education and learning

One certainty about the future is that change will be continuous and constant. A mindset that embraces continual change, and works with it, will be a required characteristic for living a happy and fulfilled life. For educationalists, this is arguably more important, as they have the responsibility of preparing and helping others to negotiate their way through a constantly changing world that at times can feel overwhelming.

From the global trends we have identified, along with their local implications, we think there may be four key elements which will shape learning and education for the future. We explore these in more detail through the four quadrants of the Schools of Tomorrow Framework in Part Two, but in summary they are:

1 *Achievement and learning for life* – To enjoy a long and fulfilled life full of constant change, we will need to embrace lifelong learning.

2 *Well-being* – When we feel good about ourselves we are more engaged and perform better. We are healthier and happier. We feel more positive and confident, and have higher aspirations. We learn better and are better able to accept and respond positively to change.

3 *Identity and agency* – Increasingly, people define and create their own identities. Individuals begin undertaking the process of identity formation from an early age, along with the development of interpersonal skills required to confidently present oneself and interact with others in the range of situations to be encountered throughout a long life. Agency means having the energy, drive, and passion to want to do things and to make a difference. It involves inquisitiveness, curiosity, and the ability to collaborate creatively, along with the willingness to learn from mistakes and the persistence to try again to achieve objectives. It applies to every aspect of life. Children need to be helped, supported, and encouraged to develop agency from birth and throughout life in order to be able to engage positively with the world.

4 *Family and communities* – Very few localities are unaffected by globalisation. The connectivity of the internet and social media means that location need no longer constrain the networks and communities to which we belong. Belonging to a community, whatever form this may take, remains important, if not essential, to us socially and emotionally. The cohesion of the society in which we live is a very important factor in providing us with a sense of safety, security, and well-being.

In the complex world of today we are constantly faced with different options and choices. This requires continuous decision-making. The values and ethics we apply to underpin our decision-making have never been so important. They are integral to the way we choose to respond to these four elements.

Conclusion to Part One

It is for school leaders to develop a local understanding of their learning context, through the engagement of all their students, parents and families, staff, communities, and local and global partners. Interpreting local and global events and changing circumstances, and examining what this means for the community and school, needs to become part of 'what and who we are' rather than a one-off exercise or something we merely touch on at regular intervals. The excitement comes from the fact that every context is new and different, whilst also being part of and connected to other localities nationally and internationally.

In Part Two of the book, we look in more detail at how some practising school leaders are pointing the way towards education and learning for the future. We will explore how five leaders, working across the whole spectrum of phases, are already considering these elements in their schools and contexts using the four-quadrant Schools of Tomorrow Framework, how they are experiencing living and leading for both the present and future, and what they are learning from this.

School leaders looking to tomorrow, whilst living in the complex, changing world of today, have to work within the confluence of global forces as well as the shifts and contradictions of national policy. It is unrealistic for school leaders to expect to be able to direct change or control exactly what happens in their school. For that reason, we think new leadership solutions, rather than structural reforms, are required, and we will examine these in more detail in Part Three.

Questions for reflection and discussion

- Which three changes happening in the world currently do you see as being most important to focus upon for education and learning in your school and community?
- How would you describe the levels of agency in the community of your school?
- How do your students and staff define their personal identities? How is this changing?
- How are families and relationships changing in your locality?

Part Two:
Towards Tomorrow

Introduction:
Building a Deeper Understanding of School Purpose and Quality in Practice – Five Leaders and Four Quadrants

At the start of this book we introduced the idea of three horizons, suggested by Curry and Hodgson (2008), to characterise responses to the challenge of establishing a sustainable energy supply. The first horizon is occupied by those who wish to continue with the present way of generating and using energy, with an over-reliance on the environmentally damaging use of fossil fuels. This is analogous of our present unsustainable model of schooling. Chapter 2 identified tensions within current education policy that continue to serve those outmoded approaches to schooling and that fail many children whilst not addressing the challenges of the changing world we inhabit.

Those on the third horizon seek to create an alternative viable solution which would meet future energy needs using sustainable sources, but this is as yet experimental and not yet scalable. In Chapter 3, we set out what we consider to be the main global factors that will have implications for education and learning in the future. The essential point here is that these global changes require a fundamental re-conception of how we understand and think about every aspect of the world in which we live. Changes in one area are changing other aspects of how we live our lives. To ignore this and to try to hold on to old certainties inevitably results in swimming against the tide, even though we may appear stationary for the time being. The challenge for school leaders is to find a way to live and lead within a second horizon, between and influenced by both the first and the third.

If we are to get a better understanding of the processes of change and of school improvement for the schools of tomorrow, then complexity theory offers a useful model. Professor Lynn Davies (2014: 12) argues that, in contrast to linear, hierarchical views of change, using a complexity mindset permits a different way of contemplating intervention. Complexity thinking requires a move from structured to organic understandings of change. It encourages us to develop an understanding of schools and their environments as complex adaptive organisms, rather than as machines or factories.

In *Leadership and the New Science*, Margaret Wheatley (2006) outlines what organisational leaders can learn from the changes that have taken place in science over the past century. What the sciences have had to come to terms with is the impossibility of making predictions based on simple causal relationships, except under very carefully controlled laboratory conditions. In the real world, other factors enter the equation, creating changes which are inconsistent, turbulent, and unpredictable. If, as individuals, we have a view of the world that is mechanistic and our aim is to control what happens around us, this can be very unsettling and disturbing, resulting in constant disappointments and feelings of failure.

However, what scientists have come to realise is that the world, despite the constant turbulence and chaos of continuous events, is orderly. More than that, natural systems will necessarily make adaptations in order to continue to exist in a constantly changing environment. A failure to do this risks entropy and demise. The essence of Wheatley's argument is that people are part of the natural world: we are not machines, 'but we live with the same forces intrinsic to all other life'. She asks us to consider what would happen 'if we stopped looking for control and began, in earnest, the search for order' (Wheatley, 2006: 25). Dynamic, natural systems could hold the answer, she suggests.

Three associated concepts seem particularly pertinent to explore to help develop our understanding of organic change; *emergence*, *connectedness*, and *feedback*. Firstly, the concept of emergence posits that, given a sufficient degree of complexity in a particular environment (and a school is an extremely complex environment), new and, in many cases, unexpected properties and behaviours will emerge. Wheatley (2006: 15) emphasises that organisations are organic, living systems and are most effective when they are open, when relationships are strong, and when people can 'exhibit self-organizing capacity'. Davies (2014: 12) also stresses the importance of 'turbulence' within an organisation for creativity to emerge. Put another way, leaders can create open, organic cultures that are dynamic and facilitate the emergence of new ways of working. Failures and mistakes are viewed as providing more information for further learning rather than as disasters to be avoided. Wheatley (2006: 39) points out that an essential role of organisations is to have clear 'organizational intent and identity', within which people contribute as team players, so that the healthy organisation is working towards the same goals.

Secondly, new properties and behaviours emerge not only from the elements that constitute a system, but also from the myriad *connections* amongst them. Such connections multiply exponentially when the environment is right. Davies (2014: 12) emphasises the importance of horizontalism, rather than top-down leadership, together with the need for networking and creating alliances. In her view, political organisation is an essential aspect of the organic organisation, with networking providing greater understanding of those holding opposing views and their motivations. Wheatley (2006: 43) observes that one of the key challenges for leaders is 'to see past the innumerable fragments to the whole' and 'to appreciate how things move and change as a coherent entity'. A key quality of leaders for tomorrow is to recognise the connections that are happening all the time and find and reinforce the 'critical connections' that have greater impact and benefit (Wheatley, 2006: 45).

Thirdly, the part played by positive feedback is crucial in this process. In Wheatley's model, information is a form of 'nourishment' (Wheatley 2006: 101, 107), but requires ability and intelligence to be processed. Wheatley (2006: 105) describes how all living beings, individuals, and organisations are continuously in the process of organising information: information which can be messy and full of random connections. Only when information is identified as 'meaningful' does it become a potent force for change. She likens these connections to fractals that are repeated and found throughout different parts of the organisation, because individuals are given information and the responsibility to use it.

Finally, information is constantly feeding back on itself. People exchange opinions, ideas, and thoughts. This creates change that is relentlessly non-linear and chaotic. As a result 'a variance that was too small to notice can cause enormous impact, far beyond anything predicted' (Wheatley, 2006: 121–122). The danger of so much information and data is that we become increasingly less able to process, understand, and identify the important, particularly qualitative, factors to which we should pay attention. In response, Wheatley (2006: 131) says that leaders are 'obligated to help the whole organization look at itself, to be reflective and learningful about its activities and decisions', and that they should help give the organisation a 'clear identity' and 'meaning'.

We will return to the theme of complexity in Part Three. It is core to our understanding of change, even though envisioning the world in this way presents those leaders who are living and leading between today and tomorrow with challenges that are risky, very scary, and which will, at times, feel overwhelming. This is especially true when considered in the context of regulatory regimes that adopt a simplistic, mechanistic approach. Within complexity thinking are some very simple messages about the importance of learning culture, participation, engagement, connectedness, and of having a clear vision, a sense of identity, and a strong culture. These form part of the second horizon which is occupied by those leaders who are trying to make sense of and navigate between the failing present, with all its tensions and contradictions, and the, as yet, uncertain future horizon in order to seek more sustainable futures for their organisations. This, we suggest, is where the real action lies.

Questions for reflection and discussion

- To what extent do you view your school and its communities as complex adaptive organisms rather than as linear systems or machines?
- In what ways is this currently reflected through its leadership? In what ways is it not?

Introducing five leaders and their schools

In this part of the book we meet five innovative school leaders who are working within this second horizon. We explore how, in their organisations and communities, their work draws on their deeper understanding of change and perhaps intuitive grasp of the intrinsic chaos of life. Finally, we explore a holistic framework for conceptualising school purpose and quality against the complexity of the modern world that schools and the young people in their charge inhabit. Wheatley identified core characteristics of those organisations and leaders that are succeeding in our chaotic, turbulent world, and we can identify many of these characteristics in the five school leaders to whom we will introduce you shortly.

We will examine their work in some detail through the lens of the four-quadrant Schools of Tomorrow Framework before offering, in Part Three, an analysis of what their leadership experience can tell us about developing new understandings of leading change for the future. Through this, we will suggest a possible way of imagining an alternative approach to school improvement and system leadership in the next phase, as the fault lines inherent in our current models become increasingly exposed.

Building your plane whilst flying it, which is essentially what second-horizon leaders are doing, is a challenging and stressful occupation. But it is also one that any number of school leaders are accomplishing on a daily basis. Here, we briefly introduce five such leaders who cover the span of nursery, primary, and secondary experience. Some serve urban communities, some more rural ones. Some work in schools which are very large, and others are in smaller settings. Some are already working within multi-academy trusts and some are in the process of forming new ones, but all have placed an equally high emphasis on meaningful collaboration with other schools as part of a local ecosystem of educational provision, which also extends beyond schooling. We will explore further the implications of their experience for the future development of MATs in Chapter 9.

Our five leaders' schools are all now rated either good or outstanding, but four required improvement when the leaders first assumed their positions, whilst one was in special measures. Although all five leaders recognised and responded to their individual school improvement imperatives, they share certain features in the ways they approached this. They did not see improvement as an end in itself. They did not look for quick fixes, but were both canny and pragmatic in pursuit of their goals. They focused on changing the culture, not the staff or the pupils, in order to allow those same individuals to fulfil their potential. Above all, they were guided not by a handbook or a manual but by a clear set of lived values. As a result, they all have a clear sense of education as being about something wider than their school; something to which their school is inextricably linked as just a part of the whole.

One of their key tools lies in the four-quadrant framework for school purpose and quality, developed in conjunction with Schools of Tomorrow. In Chapters 4 to 7 we explore the framework which has helped to shape, and has been shaped by, our leaders' thinking and approaches. We examine each of its four elements in some detail and look at how they are influencing our leaders' work using practical examples and case studies. Firstly, though, let us meet each leader and their schools in turn.

Isabel Davis

Isabel Davis became the head teacher of Peter Pan Nursery School, Bedford, in September 2012, having been deputy head from 2009 and then acting head teacher. Nursery schools in Bedford were affected by financial restructuring early in 2013, which necessitated reductions in salary costs in order to protect the provision for children. As a result, Peter Pan and the neighbouring Southway Nursery School formed a hard federation in September 2013, with Isabel as executive head teacher. Since then, and despite initial concerns about the rapid pace of these changes, Cherry Trees Nursery School has also become part of the federation, with Isabel as the executive head teacher of all three.

The three nursery schools are within walking distance of each other, serving the same part of Bedford and, as such, very similar communities. They also share, as would be expected, the same commitment to early years philosophy and common approaches, but each has their own distinct identity, culture, and ethos. These rapid changes have, inevitably, had a major impact on Isabel's role as she now leads the three nursery schools, aiming to embed a shared culture and ethos across all of them.

The children who attend the nursery schools come from a very diverse community, with many speaking English as a second language. Many families are from an Asian background and have Punjabi, Urdu, or Bengali as a first language. An increasing number of local families originally come from other parts of Europe, particularly Poland and Lithuania.

Peter Pan Nursery School was judged outstanding by Ofsted in February 2013, which Isabel attributes to always asking staff the question, 'Do you think that every child in your care is doing the very best they can?' For her, 'when we can prove that they are, then we are truly outstanding'. However, it became clear that to ensure the children were indeed 'doing the very best they can', they would need to know each child holistically, including how they are feeling and progressing emotionally and socially. This would be critical if they were to achieve their vision of enabling children to be independent, lifelong learners within their learning environment and the community.

Isabel has a very strong vision, which is remarkably evident from visiting the nursery, observing the children, or talking to staff and parents:

> What I want is children taking responsibility for their own learning, adults taking responsibility for their own learning, and parents taking responsibility for their learning and their children's. Our job is to give them the tools to be able to do that and have very high expectations of what all those children can achieve. And there aren't any limits on any of those groups of people, whatever their background or whatever they've done in the past. They can achieve really highly, and the way they do that is by having all those skills and support from their peers. Whether they are children, or adults, or parents, they need the support network around them and to know how to ask the questions of how they can improve.

What Isabel and her senior colleagues wanted was a way of building on what the nursery school had already achieved, but one which would help them to develop every child holistically and begin to provide the foundation elements for each child to grow as a learner and human being. In Chapter 5, we will look at how they went about finding that way.

Andrew Morrish

Victoria Park Primary Academy in Smethwick has 550 pupils on roll. Some 52% of these are eligible for free school meals, 93% come from a minority ethnic group, and 68% speak English as an additional language. More than 40 different languages are spoken in the school. As is the case in many urban schools which serve a deprived multicultural community, pupils come to Victoria Park with a wide range of complex needs, be it language based, behavioural, emotional, or cognitive.

In 2005, Victoria Park was placed in special measures and subsequently, after a year of interregnum, Andrew Morrish became its new head teacher. One thousand days later it was, and has remained since, an outstanding school. A fuller account of this journey is contained in his own book (Morrish, 2016).

What makes Victoria Park 'outstanding' is, in Andrew's words, 'a deeply embedded culture of creativity that will guarantee lifelong learners'; a quality that is perceived by both staff and pupils. This encompasses, but goes far beyond, Ofsted criteria. Indeed, at times along that thousand-day journey, both Her Majesty's Inspectorate and the local authority indicated that they were not especially impressed with what they were seeing. Andrew, however, did not concede, and did not fall into the trap of seeking a quick fix through knee-jerk responses. He was instead carefully laying the foundations for long-term success.

For a number of families, education is not necessarily high on their agenda. Andrew concluded:

> We had to find other ways of giving the children the tools to stand out from the rest. Of course, reading, writing and mathematics are important, and we all want to be top of the league tables. But for some schools, that's just not going to happen. So instead, we need to load the deck – to deal these pupils a hand that will allow them to hold their own in society. Teaching pupils how to be independent, confident learners who are resilient and resourceful is essential if they are to stand out in their own right.

For the last three years Victoria Park has also been an academy sponsor. Andrew is chief executive of the resulting MAT and is responsible for six primary schools across four neighbouring local authorities, totalling an intake of 2,300 children. Two of the schools in the MAT are in special measures at the time of writing; the others are rated either good or outstanding. Andrew describes the MAT as 'a family of schools for creating social entrepreneurs'. He is of course talking mainly, but not exclusively, about the pupils. That is to say, social entrepreneurship is a quality that he believes will make them truly stand out in life. In Chapter 6 we will explore some of the tools and thinking developed to underpin this vision.

Julie Taylor

The Thomas Deacon Academy (TDA) in Peterborough opened in 2007 and was one of the first academies to be created in the UK. It was, and still is, one of the largest academies in England, offering a very modern learning environment for students aged 7–18. Whilst almost half the students come from a white British background, the proportion of students from minority ethnic groups is well above the national average, with the majority of Pakistani descent. The proportion of students who do not speak English as their first language is well above the national average, as is the proportion of students supported by the pupil premium.

Julie Taylor took over as CEO and principal in September 2013, just after the school was judged to require improvement by Ofsted. This was her third headship, having previously led two much smaller, largely mono-cultural, 11–16 schools in Hampshire, including one which was in special measures. Where TDA differed was in its sheer size:

> After two or three years you know everyone in a smaller school, but that's impossible in TDA. So for me the challenge was how to deliver and quality assure the same strategies and how to ensure leaders are all operating at the same consistent level. Any inconsistency will undo good work. It was largely about introducing systems and policies and then modelling how you evidence and know they are working and affecting outcomes for young people.

Values, for Julie, are about doing the best possible job for children and families, with the belief that, 'however fractured the education system is, and however much the government tinkers with it, it is incumbent on us to step up and do the right thing for children'. Doing the right thing is not just about getting GCSE results at the expense of everything else: 'It's about making sure they know they matter as young people.'

Inheriting such a large school, Julie also realised that using the four quadrants of the Schools of Tomorrow Framework would enable her to drive through an agenda of school improvement in a way that did not create a narrow focus on GCSE outcomes: 'Although there was a clear task ahead to improve GCSE results, I felt it was important to acknowledge that school is not an end in itself but a preparation for future life.' The four quadrants gave staff a language to use outside of the Ofsted framework, which allowed them to explore what they thought was important in order to equip students to make a success of *their* future.

Within two years, the school had moved from requires improvement to good in Ofsted's terms. Having since been asked to support two other local schools in difficulties, Julie then embarked on the process of setting up a MAT. This has proved both challenging and time consuming:

> Part of the lesson I've learned to take into the MAT is that you can have the best systems and policies in the world but the personal touch still matters. You can't be a remote figure; you still have to build relationships and the community. It doesn't matter if the organisation is huge, to the organisation there's only one of you.

Julie is critical of the model that requires children and families to fit into a particular system and structure. Unity of purpose and diversity of practice has become the guiding theme behind their organisational processes.

Clive Corbett

Clive Corbett has been head teacher at Pershore High School in Worcestershire for 15 years, having first been appointed as deputy five years earlier. The school serves a rural catchment and has around 1,200 pupils on roll. It converted to single academy status in July 2011 and was inspected by Ofsted in 2013. It was judged to be good with outstanding features, specifically the behaviour and safety of pupils.

According to this inspection report almost all students are from white British backgrounds. There are no students who are at the early stages of learning English. The proportion of pupils with a disability or special educational need (SEN) supported through school action is below average. The proportion supported at school action plus level, or with a statement of SEN, is broadly average. The school has a specialist Autism Base providing tailored support for up to 15 students with autism spectrum disorder (ASD).

The report also noted that the proportion of students known to be eligible for support through the pupil premium is below average. There is additional support for children in the care of the local authority, pupils known to be eligible for free school meals, and pupils with a parent in the armed services. Some students from Key Stage 4 attend alternative provision at South Worcestershire College and the Pershore campus of Warwickshire College, where they follow vocational courses including animal care, land-based studies, motor vehicle maintenance, and hair and beauty.

Clive has seen his role at the school as being to:

> balance setting the school and the children ever higher and more demanding outcome requirements while making sure that we don't lose the focus on the well-being of the young people, and indeed the well-being of staff, and the focus on preparing young people more broadly for the future. And I think that's a continuing tension that's going to exist into the future.

The improvement strategy at Pershore is broadly conceived, with an increasing emphasis on stakeholder engagement. This has included a strong emphasis on the development of student leadership, a key feature in all five leaders' schools, and through beginning to draw staff, parents, and the wider community – as well as students – into a deeper dialogue about school priorities and progress. One of the forms this took at Pershore was a programme called learning ambassadors which will be described in detail in Chapter 6.

At the time of writing, the school was in the process of forming a MAT, interestingly with three first schools. This aims to realise the school's firm commitment to the importance of early years as laying the foundations for later learning. It is the beginning of a 10-year strategy for long-term deep-rooted improvement, but it is also about shared values and a shared vision. Part of that vision is to work with families and communities at a much earlier stage, with a focus on raising the aspirations of the children and their families.

Helen Holman

Helen Holman has been head teacher of Orchard School, Bristol, since 2006. She took up this position soon after the school was created from a former secondary school which was perceived to be failing. It is a medium-sized 11–16 school. Most students are of white British heritage, but the number of children who speak English as an additional language has been increasing rapidly in recent years. The proportion of students with SEN and the percentage known to be eligible for free school meals are above national average. There are very high levels of pupil mobility.

Orchard School serves a deprived, fragmented, and largely undefined community on the outskirts of the city. In Helen's words:

> We don't have a village centre, or a set of shops, or a church, or anything that clearly defines the community. Our parents and children don't have that in their own lives either. So, I feel our school, hopefully working with partner schools, actually has a role in defining what that community might mean.

Two local wards have very high levels of deprivation:

> I think we've the lowest average age of mortality in the city. People die younger in one ward than anywhere else in Bristol. The other has the second worst figure. That's kind of daunting. What does it mean for our community in terms of health and well-being – both their physical health and well-being as well as their mental health and well-being? It obviously impacts upon our children. I sometimes describe my children as coming from chaotic backgrounds. That could sound fun, but it's by no means fun. I have children who move from family member to family member during their schooling. Some have already been to three or four secondary schools. Not the majority, but some. This has a huge impact.

In 2015 the school was rated good by Ofsted after several years deemed to require improvement based on pupil attainment data. That had been a patient and painstaking journey:

> The improvement in this school hasn't been one sharp straight line by any stretch, and I wish it had taken less time. We hear about revolutionary changes and this hasn't been revolutionary, although I think perhaps it has in a way. It's not been rapid, but I hope it's embedded. It's not about me, it's not dependent on me, it's about confidence, and I think that goes for the community too. Some of my best conversations are with families now: it's clear the family is happy their children are here. They smile. They say 'well done'. They say good things about us. That confidence isn't about me as a leader. I don't think that's changed a lot. The confidence is in what we've created together here. Yes, the whole community. I think it's about the quality

and confidence of the community in which I work, and the confidence of this school in what it can do.

Through careful nurturing of relationships and trust-building at every level, sustained over time and in the face of adversity, change happened, and it paid dividends. Because of this increased confidence, Orchard School has been able to go on to develop strong partnerships, and we will explore these further in Chapter 7.

Overview

As a result of our study of these leaders and their work, we think their experience can help us to reach a broader and better understanding of purpose and quality in schooling, and how that can be reconciled with the limitations inherent in the first horizon. The nature of the leadership of change – in ways which serve a broader purpose, are successfully embedded, and build community confidence – is discussed in Chapter 8.

Whilst all five leaders are different in many ways, one thing they have in common is that each has simultaneously contributed to and made use of the four-quadrant Schools of Tomorrow Framework to help them achieve change. It is to the nature and use of that framework that we now turn.

Questions for reflection and discussion

Consider your own leadership journey:

- In what ways is it similar to and different from the experience of these leaders?
- What are the values which have guided it?
- Where did these values come from?
- How have you changed or developed over time?

Introducing the four-quadrant Schools of Tomorrow Framework

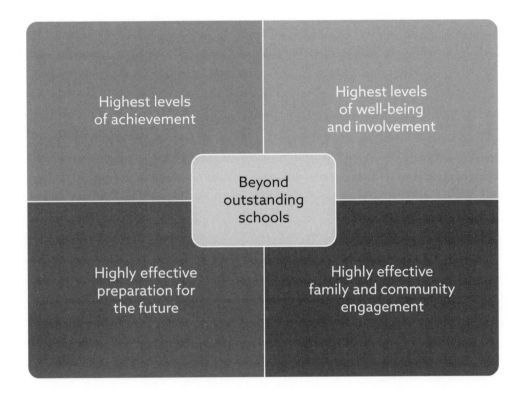

Figure 6: The four-quadrant Schools of Tomorrow Framework

In order to better understand what these five second-horizon school leaders are trying to achieve, in the next four chapters we look in some depth at each of the four quadrants in this model for school purpose and quality. The framework was developed by our five leaders, working with others through Schools of Tomorrow, initially with the aim of identifying the main qualities that encapsulated their vision and values for education. These were considered and worked on by a group of 30 or so school leaders over an 18-month period. We set out these propositions, along with some of the evidence base that informs them, in Chapter 1. As these leaders have gone on to use the framework in their schools, they have added to and developed a deeper understanding of each quadrant and, significantly, how they inherently interrelate. This is perhaps the first and most important point to note about the framework: it is a holistic model. If the four quadrants are fragmented into separate, distinct parts, then this is likely to result in a return to a mechanistic approach, rather than serve as a tool to develop deeper understanding of the complex adaptive systems within which school leaders live and work.

When used as a means to think about the four fundamentals identified in the quadrants, and consider how they are interrelated and interconnected, the framework can help to provide a basis for redefining what we mean by an outstanding school. This means actively searching for the 'critical connections' that Wheatley (2006: 45) talks about. The constituent elements that are dominant in one quadrant will always be evident in different ways, at different times, and in different contexts both within that quadrant and in connection to other elements dominant in other quadrants.

Critical connections are exciting and powerful. They can unleash forces that accelerate and magnify change, particularly when groups are trusted and empowered with the responsibility to take the connections forward. The leader's role becomes one of facilitating and enabling, ensuring consistency to the core vision, values, and identity of the whole system. We have outlined how Wheatley describes the repetition of complex patterns and shapes found throughout an organisation as being part of a fractal world. The paradox is how differences are found throughout the system, but with recognisable shapes and patterns that can be found at different levels.

The framework also allows for the fact that outstanding in one community context may appear very different in another, whilst outcomes for children and young people will be defined not simply in terms of a limited measure of things they have (or haven't) achieved at set points of time in the past, but in terms of how well their learning prepares them to meet, understand, and shape their future.

In the next four chapters, we explore the experiences of these five leaders and their understanding of the framework in their schools' context. We use a combination of research-informed analysis and accounts of changes in practice in relation to each of the four quadrants, whilst recognising that the quadrants are essentially interlinked. One of the critical roles of leadership is to grasp and exploit these interconnections.

One further consequence of this interconnection is that the next four chapters are not linear and sequential, and you may want to take account of that in the way you decide to read them. They can be tackled in any order, and your choice may reflect both your interests and the circumstances of your own journey. Working within the limitations of a linear book format, we had to decide upon the order in which to describe the four quadrants. However, we challenge you not to accept the sequence as prescribed by us, but to set your own order for reading, analysing, and responding to the ideas within each chapter. Perhaps avoid starting with the quadrant that feels most familiar to you or reflects your current priorities: be bolder and move out of your comfort zone! If in doubt, select an order at random and see where it takes you. And better still, read and discuss the chapters with others as you will inevitably learn more collectively.

Questions for reflection and discussion

- How would you, at this moment, view the ideal balance between these four elements?
- In practice, is that view the same as your school's view?
- What interconnections can you see?
- Where is your starting point for change going to be?

Chapter 4

The Achievement Quadrant

At interview, I was asked how I was going to improve KS2 SATs results as the school's number one priority. I said: 'Actually, it's not the priority. If you want me to improve KS2 SATs results, then the last thing I'm going to do is improve KS2 SATs results. I'm going to do it by getting into nursery and reception, by getting into Year 1, and changing things there. Come and judge me in seven years' time.' It was good the governing body understood that. They put trust in me, and they took a risk in appointing me. I vowed I'd pay that back.

Andrew Morrish

The first and most important point to note is that the focus of this quadrant is *achievement* and not *attainment*. Education policy in the UK and in other countries has for many years placed an almost exclusive focus on measuring particular types of attainment, with the result that we can lose sight of the distinction between achievement and attainment, and of the fact that achievement is many things.

Achievement *is* many things. Some of these are rightly and properly defined by the government. It is their role to determine, in part, the nature of the return society expects for its investment in schools. There may, of course, be better or worse ways for the government to define achievement. That is a matter for proper and informed debate, in which schools themselves are not the only or main contributor, despite having something important to say. Equally, frequent changes in definition and policy – often for no apparent good reason – are not helpful educationally and have not contributed to an informed debate. Hopefully you will already have asked yourself, 'What do we mean by achievement?' Which begs a second question, 'Who do we mean by "we"?'

Defining achievement is not easy because it is multifaceted. It needs to have elements that are personalised to the individual, recognising that people progress at different ages and rates, and find some aspects of learning easier than others. Comparisons of attainment should not necessarily be equated with comparisons of achievement. Thus, achievement also needs to be defined by and with the learner, in terms of their individual hopes and aspirations. Of course, these are not absolute either, for it is part of the educator's role to help lift aspirations that have been limited by experience or opportunity. This requires a partnership of trust, not an imposition of values.

Megan was a Year 11 student at Clive Corbett's school when we spoke to her as part of our research. She talks here about her school experience:

In secondary school, children are not seen as individuals. You become part of a system. I realised I didn't want to be seen as a number. I wanted to work out a healthy balance between being a person and getting good grades. Before, it was like teachers were saying to us 'you need to get the grades Year 11 got last year'. But through our work with Schools of Tomorrow and the four-quadrant framework, we were able to speak to the head and teachers about this. Now in assembly, for instance, they say to us 'you need to do your best'. Simple things, just changing words, but it's really, really helpful. I want to be treated as a human being who's here to learn, not just get exam grades.

Yet Megan was attending a good school, one whose outstanding ethos had been praised by Ofsted in 2013, when they reported:

> Students have good attitudes to learning and behave exceptionally well around the school. They have impeccable manners and are extremely welcoming and polite to visitors. Students are proud to attend the school and many were keen to tell inspectors how much they are enjoying their time there. ... An outstanding feature of the school's work is the way in which it promotes the development of leadership skills amongst students. (Ofsted, 2013: 5)

What had happened here was that Megan had developed her own view of what achievement looked like for her. And the school, to its credit, listened carefully and took this on board more widely, making subtle but important changes – for example, in the language staff used when talking with students.

Most of us will live long lives characterised by constant change in every aspect, from the personal to the global. Embracing a life of learning will be essential to our enjoyment and fulfilment. To have an enquiring mind throughout one's life – a mind that constantly asks questions, seeks new challenges, and creatively engages with others, with ideas, and with the world – involves habits and mindsets that need to be embedded and maintained from the early years onwards.

Evidence from our five leaders suggests that emerging schools of tomorrow share a number of common characteristics that help establish the foundations for lifelong learning:

- *A learning culture* – A learning culture regards all students, staff, and adults as learners: everyone is subject to the same high expectations that they improve performance, learn from experience, collaborate, and support each other. All, as learners, are expected and supported to reflect upon and learn from experience, with research by both students and staff a core component of practice.

- *A common language of learning* – Victoria Park Primary Academy adopted the term *learnish* for their language of learning, which is used consistently from the early years upward. Students quickly acquire the language and become at ease with complex concepts (e.g. metacognition) and what they mean for their learning. A shared language of learning is synonymous with a learning culture and also helps to develop personal responsibility and independence of learning.

- *Extended and community learning* – There is a danger that the term 'lifelong learning' has become a hackneyed phrase to which people pay lip service but give no meaning. The five schools demonstrate different interpretations of what it can mean in their context through their practice. This frequently involves extending students' learning beyond the school, engaging parents and other adults in the learning of students, or encouraging adults in the community to extend their own learning. Reconceptualising how and where learning can take place within communities, and the role of local educational provision to lead and support this, is one of the greatest challenges in developing extended learning cultures.

Change study 1: Moving from Ofsted's requires improvement to good

Julie Taylor used the four-quadrant framework, in conjunction with the four areas of Ofsted's inspection framework, as a foundation for leading TDA out of the 'requires improvement' category. This allowed staff, students, parents, and governors to articulate and develop a much clearer vision of what they valued about TDA and the kind of education they wanted to see it offer. It encouraged the range of stakeholders to agree a set of values on which to base all decisions and to develop a collective vision of what they wanted for themselves and for the wider school community. As a result, TDA's improvement plan was highly ambitious and led to the need to totally reorganise the structure of the academy.

Whilst the achievement quadrant was an important focus, Julie wanted to develop what was for her a key missing component at TDA: highly effective family and community engagement. Julie's previous two headships had taught her the benefit of successful engagement with the wider community, and she knew that this aspect, crucially often overlooked by struggling schools, would prove a key component in school improvement. Julie approached a member of her senior leadership team (SLT) with the task of completely rethinking the ways in which TDA engaged with families and the wider community.

The resulting plan not only included some very practical aspects – like developing a successful parents' forum, and working parties comprised of parents, students, and teachers – but also focused on building and maintaining a TDA international student programme. Additionally, establishing a STEM scholarship programme – designed to encourage students to consider further study and careers in science, technology, engineering, and maths – enabled TDA to engage effectively with higher education and business.

Julie has witnessed first-hand the benefits for students but has also noted the improvement in TDA's reputation in the community:

> Local people did not feel that they were part of what was happening at TDA. By working more openly with the community and with parents, they understand better what we are trying to achieve for the children and young people. As a result, they criticise less and help more.

TDA serves a very ethnically diverse community and the academy's chairman, Dr Richard Barnes, is clear that the engagement quadrant of the Schools of Tomorrow Framework remains a high priority if it is to continue to improve. He believes that greater community engagement will bring greater success for TDA students and their families.

At the end of her first year at TDA, it was clear to Julie that there needed to be a complete reconsideration of both the staffing structure and the ways in which students were organised, if standards were to improve. Reflecting on the well-being and future quadrants, Julie decided that there needed to be clearer systems for supporting both academic achievement and student well-being within the academy's structures. When Julie took over TDA, she inherited a collegiate system; each of the six colleges within the academy had its own college leader who was responsible for pastoral welfare as well as attainment and progress for specific groups of subjects. Whilst the collegiate model of pastoral support was sound, the blurred lines of accountability for standards and progress had seen TDA sitting below the standards that are accepted as 'national average' academically. Using the Schools of Tomorrow Framework as the underpinning model, Julie redesigned TDA's staffing structure (including teaching and non-teaching staff) to enable a definite line to be drawn between accountability for curriculum and academic standards and responsibility for pastoral support.

At the heart of this, Julie placed her commitment to the well-being of students and staff, creating a structure and realignment of accountability which would allow students to be supported well and bring greater clarity to the roles and responsibilities of members of staff:

> There was an overwhelming sense of 'thank goodness' from staff, students and parents. Bringing greater clarity to the organisational structure has led to a real belief in well-being: if students are supported well, they will be able to achieve the best they can.

This is a good example of a 'critical connection' being made. One unforeseen outcome of using the Schools of Tomorrow Framework that Julie has noted is that, even at times of extreme pressure during the process of reorganisation, it has given senior leaders and staff a positive structure to talk about school improvement:

> Being in a 'requires improvement' category meant, at times, staff felt forced to focus on a narrow set of data that neither told the whole story of education at TDA, nor allowed staff and students to develop what mattered to them.

Julie believes the four-quadrant framework enabled staff and students not to lose sight of what was important. As a result of adhering to these principles, staff and students had the resilience to face Ofsted's re-inspection in July 2015, which resulted in a 'good' judgement. This, coupled with another set of improved examination results in August 2015, provides a clear example of the framework's success. Julie recognises that this is only the beginning of the journey at TDA, and that the Schools of Tomorrow Framework will be critical not only in consolidating the work undertaken so far but also in developing a quality culture as the academy continues to progress and develops its own MAT.

The next challenge for TDA is to achieve a greater understanding of the power of the interconnections between the quadrants, not only amongst governors and school leaders but also students, parents, and the wider community:

As the CEO and principal, I am ambitious, with a clear sense of purpose for the children and young people who attend our academy, but you have to have a balanced view that values the needs of both the individuals and the wider community. As teachers and adults working with young people, it is those great qualities of self-confidence, perseverance, openness to new ideas, and readiness to take the initiative and to innovate that will enable our students to achieve both inside and outside the classroom, and it is our responsibility as adults to model those qualities to our students.

Redefining quality and purpose

A redefinition of school quality and purpose is implicit in the use of the four-quadrant framework. However, the measurements around quality and purpose, as well as the forms of measurement used, need to be taken carefully to reflect that change. 'Don't value what you measure, measure what you value' may be an old adage, but is one that is all too often neglected in the world of education today. Measurement is important, and data is really valuable, but the purpose needs to be clear. As this change study suggests, securing the highest levels of achievement is not best accomplished through a narrow focus, and does not need to be at the expense of broader purposes.

For the leaders of these schools of tomorrow, the indicators used by government and inspectors to judge success inevitably have a part to play. However, these criteria need to be understood and used carefully, and they only ever tell a part of the whole story. More than that, any target indicator could actually be damaging and counter-productive through its unintended consequences. As Strathern's (1997: 308) succinct rephrasing of Goodhart's (1975: 96) law puts it, 'When a measure becomes a target, it ceases to be a good measure.' That is why, for example, at Stafford Hospital a managerial obsession with meeting government targets in order to secure foundation status for the hospital resulted in abuses of patient care and false data entries by nurses in order to seem to comply (see *The Telegraph*, 2013).

We believe it is important for each school to develop – from reflecting on its values, vision, and context – a small number of preferred indicators for measuring progress. The purpose of these is not to make judgements about success or failure but to support the asking of good questions about the rate and direction of travel. These indicators should be chosen and set by the school itself, but in turn be subject to some form of external moderation. We do not have a fixed view about their number, but think that a carefully chosen few are usually best. Choosing one indicator related to each of the four quadrants may be a useful starting point. They should also be chosen so as to 'pull' in different directions to avoid the risk of distortion of purpose which is always inherent in target-setting (Deming, 2000: 31).

Margaret Wheatley (2006: 65) makes a similar point about measurement when she says, 'no form of measurement is neutral. Every act of measurement loses more information than it gains.' Quantitative data should always be accompanied by a big health warning: recognise its limitations and identify and make use of at least some of the other information that is available. For example, observations are also important, as are the interpretations given to them. 'Hard' quantitative data is often seen as having greater value and status than such 'soft' qualitative data, but it is equally possible that hard data can lose sight of the student as a person, their progress, and their all-round development.

A measurement is an observation that quantitatively reduces uncertainty. Measurements might not yield precise, certain results, though they can help to reduce uncertainty. The object of measurement must be described clearly, in terms of what we are seeking to observe. Even if you cannot measure exactly what you want, you can learn about your area of interest with related data. A business may not be able to measure the exact benefit of a happy customer, for example, but it could get measures which give evidence of the value and magnitude of its work. It could also get measures of the cost of dissatisfied customers.

But as with all measures, you must use judgement. The danger is that we mistake the measure for the thing itself. Measures are a proxy, and we need to understand the limitations of the data we use. We should not just pretend that the data we have tells us everything we need to know. We need to think. We need to understand. The data is useful, but its limitations must equally be borne in mind.

Hubbard (2010: 32) makes four points that may be valuable for school leaders to remember when deciding how to draw upon data:

1   Your problem is not as unique as you think.

2   You have more data than you think.

3   You need less data than you think.

4   An adequate amount of new data is more accessible than you think.

Julie Taylor sums up her experience:

> People do a lot of tasks around checking this, measuring that, but don't draw it all together. You have to start to get people to work in an evidence-based way. When I started headship, I didn't understand data; I thought it was pretty useless. I didn't interrogate it, analyse it, didn't know what I was looking for. Many leaders pretend they know but don't. They never triangulate, they never relate it to the classroom day to day, so it doesn't empower them to take further action. My favourite words when looking at data are 'so what?'
>
> Once my leadership team were trained up, understood data, and used it, it was enlightening for them. They had never been trained so didn't understand why data was gathered. They thought they just provided it for Ofsted. They didn't understand it was essential for school improvement to gather good quality data, understand it, action plan from it, attach a budget to it for the next level of activity to secure real improvement. I kept things tight until people got that light bulb moment. Some got there quickly, some needed longer. I used my vice-principal to model and work alongside other leaders, and talk it through with them. It was really painful for some. There were tears, tantrums, and dark days when the easiest thing would have been to do it yourself. You have to persevere and take people through that pain barrier. Then you

reach a tipping point, with the majority working in that way, so you can start to pair people up, use co-coaching, and then you're getting there.

Conclusion

The achievement quadrant challenges school leaders to step away from the familiar focus on measures of attainment and to ask, 'What do we mean by achievement?' The answers, we suggest, lie in a much more rounded and holistic view of personal and social development. This, in turn, results in a reconsideration of purpose and of how we measure and evaluate effectiveness, progress, and success. It also makes evident the many critical connections with the dominant aspects of the other quadrants that help in finding the fractals – the patterns and shapes – that will become repeated throughout the school and its learning community.

Questions for reflection and discussion

- With whom is it important that you discuss the meaning of achievement? How will you do this?
- What does achievement mean in your school and community?
- What measures of achievement will you use?
- What data to measure achievement do you have available in your school and community? How could you make more use of it?

Chapter 5
The Well-being Quadrant

We know that academic success on its own is not enough because we know that there are some children who are doing really well, above national averages, but their well-being is really low. That's not good enough. On the performance tables it looks great, but as human beings, and as young learners, it's not enough.

Isabel Davis

As highlighted in the Introduction to Part One, in the UK we do not have an outstanding recent track record in terms of the well-being of our children. In 2007, UNICEF data placed the UK consistently near the bottom of all measures across six dimensions of children's well-being, except for health and safety. More recent data from the Children's Society's 2015 *Good Childhood Report*, which provides detailed information about how children and young people in the UK feel about their lives and about the future, shows levels of satisfaction with life as a whole may have declined. Since 2008 children aged 10–15 reported being generally less happy, although this seems to have settled in more recent years, with only around 7–8% stating low levels of general happiness (Pople et al., 2015: 17). However, overall, 'children in England had relatively low levels of subjective well-being compared to a diverse range of 14 countries' (Pople et al., 2015: 61). One worrying finding for UK educationalists is that, compared with other countries in the survey, 'children in England tended not to like going to school and reported poor relationships with teachers' (Pople et al., 2015: 56), again placing England near the bottom of international comparisons. Around 20% of the children surveyed showed signs of mental ill-health (Pople et al., 2015: 29).

Whilst well-being is clearly a matter of social concern to some degree, does this matter at all in terms of education? The relationship between well-being and educational achievement is becoming increasingly well understood, at least in research terms if not in policy. In a 2012 research report for the Department for Education entitled *The Impact of Pupil Behaviour and Wellbeing on Educational Outcomes*, Gutman and Vorhaus examined the predictive power of four dimensions of well-being – emotional, behavioural, social, and school – at three average age points: 7.5, 10.5, and 13.8 years. Their control variables included whether English was the first language, and whether the child was eligible for free school meals or identified as having SEN, along with factors such as highest parental educational level, parents' marital status, child's birth weight in grams, gender, and ethnicity. The outcome measures were academic achievement and school engagement.

Their study used data from the Avon Longitudinal Study of Parents and Children (ALSPAC) which began following 14,000 pregnant women in the west of England during 1991 and 1992. They use parent-reported data as the only consistent measure of well-being available to span the period from childhood to adolescence, but combine this with key stage scores obtained from the National Pupil Database, matched to control variables from annual school census data.

Gutman and Vorhaus used this analysis to examine the association between the four dimensions of well-being (emotional, behavioural, social, and school) at ages 7 to 13, and concurrent (i.e. measured at the same age) and later educational outcomes at ages 11 to 16, including academic achievement (i.e. national exam scores) and school engagement (i.e. being stimulated by school).

The authors summarise their key findings thus:

- Children with higher levels of emotional, behavioural, social, and school well-being, on average, have higher levels of academic achievement and are more engaged in school, both concurrently and in later years.

- Children with better emotional well-being make more progress in primary school and are more engaged in secondary school.

- Children with better attention skills experience greater progress across the four key stages of schooling in England. Those who are engaged in less troublesome behaviour also make more progress and are more engaged in secondary school.

- Children who are bullied are less engaged in primary school, whereas those with positive friendships are more engaged in secondary school.

- As children move through the school system, emotional and behavioural well-being become more important in explaining school engagement, while demographic and other characteristics become less important.

- Relationships between emotional, behavioural, social, and school well-being and later educational outcomes are generally similar for children and adolescents, regardless of their gender and parents' educational level. (Gutman and Vorhaus, 2012: 3–4)

Before considering some of the case study evidence that addresses the question of well-being in practice, we should consider how we define the term. At its most basic level, we need to take account of physical well-being, which can encompass diet, clothing, exercise, housing, physical safety, and security. Many schools have found that introducing initiatives to improve this aspect – providing breakfast clubs, encouraging children to drink water regularly, changing the lunch menu, and introducing regular daily exercise – has an immediate improvement on concentration and involvement in school. It is also important to make the critical connection between establishing these basic 'good habits' and sustaining a long, healthy, and active life. There are significant social differences in life expectancy and satisfaction associated with what we can term 'healthy living', the foundations of which are laid in childhood and adolescence.[1]

Well-being is much more than this, however. Researchers in the field of positive psychology have suggested that well-being is best characterised as a profile of indicators across multiple domains, rather than as a single factor. Seligman (2011: 15) argues that well-being cannot be defined by a single measure, but is comprised of various aspects that are more readily measured. He also warns

---

1   See, for example, http://www.agingsocietynetwork.org/differences-in-life-expectancy.

that unidimensional measures, such as life satisfaction, are strongly affected by a person's mood at the time and ignore other aspects of well-being. In fact, he notes that multidimensional measures of well-being are only moderately correlated with life satisfaction.

Seligman also considers the practical use that schools should make of assessments of well-being, stating that specific information about domains in which students thrive or struggle are more inform-ative and useful than comparative global assessments. To this end, he devised, with colleagues, the PERMA model of flourishing (Seligman, 2011: 16), which defines psychological well-being in terms of five domains:

P *Positive emotions* – refers to hedonic feelings of happiness (e.g. feeling joyful, content, and cheerful).

E *Engagement* – refers to psychological connection to activities or organisations (e.g. feeling absorbed, interested, and engaged in life).

R *Positive relationships* – includes feeling socially integrated, cared about and supported by others, and satisfied with one's social connections.

M *Meaning* – refers to believing that one's life is valuable and feeling connected to something greater than oneself.

A *Accomplishment* – involves making progress towards goals, feeling capable of doing daily activities, and having a sense of achievement.

Seligman maintains that these five pillars contribute to overall well-being, are important areas that people pursue for their own sake, and can be defined and measured independently of one another. Some aspects of the model are measured subjectively by self-report, other aspects can be measured objectively. Seligman sees student well-being as multidimensional, on both the positive and negative sides of the mental health continuum. He argues that a multidimensional approach allows schools to tailor systematic well-being approaches to the developmental needs of students. This analysis suggests that schools need to have both a detailed knowledge and understanding of the overall well-being of students, their families, and the wider community, and a means of systematically assessing the individual needs of students using a multidimensional approach.

As part of the background to preparing this chapter, during 2016 we carried out some small-scale evaluations in nine schools in Bedford which had placed a particular focus on developing a school well-being strategy. This strategy was part of a local authority initiative, overseen by Peter Pan Teach-ing School Alliance. It was informed by Seligman's model and drew on the work of a range of national partners, including Early Excellence,[2] specifically using the Leuven Scales for Emotional Well-being and Involvement, which we will outline in more detail later, and YoungMinds, especially their academic resilience framework.[3]

---

2   See http://earlyexcellence.com/.
3   See https://youngminds.org.uk/media/1465/what-is-academic-resilience.pdf.

The evaluation tracked the development of the work of the schools over a 12-month period. Whilst the well-being of pupils and how this linked to their educational achievement was the prime concern, it quickly became clear to several of the schools that the well-being of their staff, and of pupils' parents, were inextricably intertwined with the well-being and achievement of pupils. For many, though not all, of the schools, their involvement in this initiative led to significant changes in thinking, policy, and practice. At the heart of these changes lay a refocusing on the centrality of each child: understanding their specific needs and barriers to learning, then addressing these directly and personally at the earliest possible opportunity.

Common key features of the resulting changes, identified in the evaluation report (Groves, 2016), are:

- A focus on earlier identification of difficulties experienced by children, within the school and outside, and timely responses.
- The encouragement of more personalised responses which match interventions to the child rather than the other way around.
- Taking time to get to know pupils as individuals and responding to their interests and concerns.

The evaluation suggests the impact of such changes may be seen in:

- A reduction in crisis interventions leading to more productive use of staff time, both teaching and non-teaching.
- A reduction in behaviour incidents in terms of frequency and severity.
- Increased confidence and awareness amongst children.
- More effective learning by pupils.
- Improvements in staff levels of well-being with consequent reductions in staff absence and turnover.
- Supportive responses from parents.
- Tentative initial evidence of an effect on achievement in the early years in one primary school.

Of course, it was not possible to assign direct causality to any of these Bedford findings in such a way as to link these effects directly to the well-being initiative. But it is worth noting that several schools reported similar things happening. However, the potential significance of the last finding may be supported by as yet unpublished initial findings from an analysis of 500,000 baseline assessments by Early Excellence in 2016, which are suggesting a significant correlation between high levels of well-being and higher total outcomes in communication and language, literacy, and maths.

There is also no single 'right' approach for any school to take. Context is important and makes a difference. It is for each school to work out what approach is right for them at a particular time, whilst being very clear about their overall direction of travel. Dylan Wiliam (2006: 13) captured this truth well when he said:

In education, 'what works?' is not the right question because everything works somewhere and nothing works everywhere, so what's interesting, what's important in education, is 'under what conditions does this work?'

The sort of impact that several case study head teachers reported in this study did not arise from creating another initiative or project, bolted on to existing workloads. Well-being needed to be rooted at a much deeper level. As one head teacher said:

A focus on well-being has to be part of a central vision for the school, and at the heart of what you do, for it to be as effective as it has been for us.

Those heads who saw that well-being needed to be central, and acted with that in mind, were equally clear about the centrality of high levels of well-being to high levels of achievement:

If you don't address well-being, you won't get the best results. A child who is secure and happy is one who learns – and thrives as a whole individual.

But that in turn required reconceptualising how their schools worked, as one deputy head suggested:

We have I think, as a profession, got it wrong in our response to children experiencing barriers to learning. The standard response if a child is struggling in learning maths or English has been to give extra maths and English, more of the same. But if teaching is high quality, then the barrier lies elsewhere. So look for that barrier and remove it first. And it's often to do with emotional readiness to learn. That's why we've put such hefty investment into training around emotional well-being, resilience, and inclusion – to get that right.

Change study 2: Promoting the well-being of all

Isabel Davis first became involved with Schools of Tomorrow as a member of its Well-Being Working Group. At the time, well-being was a strategic priority for her emerging Bedford Federation of Nursery Schools, but she recognised in the four quadrants of the Schools of Tomorrow Framework those features she considers to be the most important part of quality teaching and learning. Almost immediately she decided to make practical use of it:

I didn't want the four-quadrant framework to be an add-on ... another thing that staff were having to think about, or another thing we were trialling for a year, but to make it part of what we were already doing.

For Isabel, it is always important to keep Ofsted in mind, so she decided to use the four quadrants as the four main areas of the federation's learning plan and to 'make the four Ofsted inspection areas fit in with each one'. In the federation's learning plan, the four quadrants related to Ofsted's (then current) criteria as follows:

- The achievement quadrant relates to Ofsted's outcomes for children and learners.
- The well-being quadrant incorporates what Ofsted includes under personal development, behaviour, and welfare.
- The preparation for the future quadrant incorporates what Ofsted includes under teaching, learning, and assessment.
- The family and community engagement quadrant includes Ofsted's effectiveness of leadership and management.

One of the main benefits of this approach was incorporating a much broader definition and shared understanding of what will achieve continuous improvement into the strategic development of the federation – an understanding which informs their planning to move beyond 'outstanding' as defined by Ofsted.

As the strategic plan was structured using the four quadrants, the understanding and thinking of governors developed with the same perspective. Governors' reports are structured using the four headings which form the strategic priorities. These are then easily incorporated as updates to the federation's self-evaluation form. Since April 2015 the sub-committees of the governing body have also been structured around the four quadrants, with terms of reference defined by each of the four priorities.

The four quadrants are used as the starting point for all self-evaluation and to help the schools identify what needs doing to secure greater improvement. It is the practice across the federation to continuously evaluate, based on evidence from a wide range of sources, including classroom observations, data, take-up of parental workshops, and a consideration of the long-term sustainability of the school.

The strapline for the federation is 'Every child's choice counts'. Training days have explored what that means for the individual child, for the nursery school, and for families. Just as staff are expected to take responsibility for themselves and to make choices, so the same principle is extended to the children and their parents. Children are given choices but are then held accountable for them, expected to 'stick by them', and then reflect on the consequences and outcomes.

Perhaps the most priceless outcome from using the Schools of Tomorrow Framework is that, in Isabel's words:

> People are happy and relaxed and can talk openly about their issues and about their problems and can disclose things if they need to.

Isabel believes this would not be the case if they had just applied the Ofsted inspection framework. Another key outcome is the way in which they now consider their communities as part of the leadership resource available for the school, and look for ways in which families can contribute to and shape the schools' direction of travel.

The focus on well-being has meant that they have moved a long way beyond just considering the behaviour and safety of pupils, as required by the Ofsted rubric. They recognise that it is essential to consider how people talk to and behave towards each other – adult to adult, adult to child, child to child. In Isabel's view:

> If that is right, then behaviour and safety will be really, really good because people are well in their skin.

Using the well-being quadrant as an example, Isabel described how the federation's starting point had been to consider this from a child's point of view. However, it quickly became apparent that valuing the highest levels of well-being for staff should also be part of the approach. Consequently, the federation's appraisal system was adapted to make sure that well-being was one of the targets. Each member of staff sets a target in relation to their personal well-being, which is then reviewed at the end of the year. Staff are expected to be able to describe what they have done to ensure that they are even more engaged, have high levels of well-being, and low levels of sickness. In Isabel's view, if the well-being of each member of staff is high, then they will achieve their other performance targets because 'they are feeling so good about themselves, about the school, and about the children'.

As this approach to appraisal was introduced, Isabel found that staff were thinking about the well-being of their colleagues before their own, saying things like, 'I know if I do this, it is going to make that person feel better, and then I will have an easier time as they are not going to be feeling so stressed.' The caring and collaborative values of the federation, and the principle of accepting personal responsibility both for oneself and for others, have been extended by staff through their focus on well-being. Isabel also observes that:

> Staff use the language of well-being and involvement, but they are also beginning to use the four-quadrant language as well.

By using that language, they not only develop understanding but also begin to apply the Schools of Tomorrow Framework in their discussions and in practice. Isabel believes that by applying the quadrants they are making:

> deeper and deeper improvements to our performance such that we are going to outperform any criteria that Ofsted may give to us.

In using the framework, staff have also come to recognise the interconnections between the four quadrants, which can operate in different ways. One example is purposefully creating different environments to achieve different outcomes. However, consistent across the federation are environments that are welcoming, safe, encourage engagement and collaboration, give choice and support, and stimulate learning.

Another example is how using the Leuven Scales for Emotional Well-being and Involvement has affected views of achievement. These scales have been developed over several years by Professor

Ferre Laevers of Leuven University in Belgium (Laevers, 2003).[4] They are designed to assess, by observation, the level of children's well-being and involvement but have also been applied in other contexts (e.g. to assess elderly people.) The five-point scales outline descriptors of different behaviours, against which the observer makes a judgement. These are then collated to give an overall assessment of the well-being and involvement of the child. Comparing the well-being and involvement ratings from the Leuven scales with children's attainment scores has provided a much more well-balanced view of achievement, and has actually resulted in improvements in attainment.

What is making the real difference is how the scales are being used. Early Excellence provided initial training for all the staff, but it is the way that this has been taken up, and is being consistently applied, that is bringing about the transformation. Lesley Boyle, deputy head for the federation, explains that as early years professionals they have always used observation as part of making assessments, but involvement in the project has meant they have now taken their practice that little bit deeper. They have become aware that even children who look busy may not be engaged in high-level learning. As Lesley says:

> When you watch what is happening with that child, the child is quite distracted, is looking around, there is a little bit of time-wasting, not really focusing, not really concentrating.

The training has involved them improving their observational skills and working together to moderate each other's assessments and judgements. Lesley describes how they 'sometimes have very heated discussions about whether it is a Level 4 or a 5', for example, and how this 'really does help us learn from each other'. The common language and perspective that has developed from this rigorous approach has contributed to increased consistency in assessments and judgements.

When the assessments identify a cause for concern, interventions are planned. These can include additional programmes for the child and family support. Continual monitoring ensures that further interventions are made until improvement in the child's well-being and involvement is observed. The well-being data is also used to review the design of the learning environment to ensure that it facilitates different learning objectives and supports the well-being of the children.

As Isabel explains:

> Whenever we change an environment or type of pedagogy we use, we look to see whether it has made a difference, whether children are responding to it, and whether it fits in with our overall ethos and our understanding of how children learn. If something doesn't work, we don't carry on doing it, even if it's something that everyone else is doing nationally. If we feel it isn't having an impact, we wouldn't do it.

Isabel describes the preparation for the future quadrant as being really enlightening for staff. It makes them consider what they are preparing children for, and think about how to develop children's confidence in their approach to life skills, helping each other, and playing an active part in their learning. Isabel believes that if they are focusing on doing that in their teaching, then everything

---

4   For a summary see http://www.earlylearninghq.org.uk/earlylearninghq-blog/the-leuven-well-being-and-involvement-scales/.

else will follow. She aims to ensure that all children know how to take turns, listen to each other in a conversation, and are confident enough to say, 'I've done this before and I know how to do this, and now I want to know how to do that.' When they have this ability, then they can take their own learning forward.

Teaching in the federation is not just expected to be outstanding but ever-improving, so the children can also continue to improve. As a consequence, there is an emphasis on staff taking responsibility for their own learning, supported by a range of professional development opportunities, including peer-to-peer coaching, continual staff training, and peer-shadowing across the federation. All this activity is underpinned by a focus on values and an expectation that lifelong learning applies to everyone. Isabel suggests that one reason why some schools never get to outstanding is because the Ofsted criteria are too narrow. Using the Schools of Tomorrow Framework is much fuller and richer, and provides a basis for producing the evidence to show that the work of the school is 'truly outstanding'.

Becoming the head of the federation has convinced Isabel that improvement will only come from all staff contributing their very best and constantly seeking to improve their performance to do their upmost for every child. Professional development is the responsibility of each individual. Isabel's role is to make sure staff are provided with the support and resources they require. In her words:

> Every day as a member of staff you have to think, 'Have I given these children the best possible chances to do their very, very best?' If you can answer that question with 'yes', then you have done a good job. For me as a leader, if I know that every child has made the best progress they can, then I am doing my job and my staff are doing the best they can. If they are not, I take it as my responsibility to show them, to help them, to be able to do that. So it is all interlinked really.

Conclusion

Well-being affects achievement in different ways and to varying degrees at different stages of learning and development. Low levels of well-being affect individual performance, and in turn that of the groups to which individuals belong. Schools need to develop a deep understanding of the well-being of students and their families, and the communities in which they are situated, and have a systematic method for doing this. This requires a multidimensional approach to methodically and rigorously assessing the well-being of individual students, with a range of intervention strategies ready to implement in response to identified needs.

School leaders and staff will develop a deeper and better understanding and be able to find and enact more effective solutions by actively involving students. Staff will have a greater awareness and will take more responsibility for their own well-being and performance because of this increased awareness of student well-being.

Questions for reflection and discussion

- How would you describe the well-being context of your school or organisation? How can you develop a deeper understanding of current well-being levels?
- What are the two most important well-being issues to affect the learning and achievement of your students? What could be done differently to effectively improve their well-being?
- How do you systematically assess the well-being of individual students?
- What intervention strategies do you use to personalise interventions to support the well-being of students and their families?
- To what extent do staff in your school take responsibility for their own well-being and support each other?

Chapter 6

The Preparation for the Future Quadrant

Our curriculum is skills-based, and based on enquiry and fascination and engagement. It's about children asking questions, about us encouraging them, facilitating and supporting their learning, and ensuring that children don't ever stop asking questions, because research shows that the average nursery-aged child asks 400 questions a day, but by the age of 7 they stop asking the questions because they know they don't get answered. Then they become compliant and just listen and wait to be told the information. For us that is absolutely terrible. So for us it's about keeping that inquisitive sense that we know is a characteristic of really good learners. To be a really good learner you've got to ask the questions and want to always find out more, and never settle for just one answer or one opinion. So that's what we really aim to do, and we base our teaching and learning on that.

Isabel Davis

The future is not something that is done to us, but an ongoing process in which we can intervene.

Keri Facer (2011: 6)

The ten global change trends identified in Chapter 3 have significant implications for the future of education and learning, but they require further analysis to progress from being a very long list of interrelated questions for us to consider. Indeed, that analysis could result in little more than further questions being generated. One of the major challenges here is that it is essential for educators to *think about* and *do* things *differently*, rather than necessarily do different things. There are important areas of social and educational development that are frequently ignored, and aspects of school which, despite being common to current practice, do not prepare people for a happy, healthy, and fulfilled long life. Recognising these factors as detrimental to learning and removing them will in itself be a major step forward.

Being at ease with a life of change

We began Chapter 3 by suggesting that one certainty about the future is that it will bring complex, interrelated changes that will affect all aspects of everyone's lives. Importantly, most changes will be unknown and unpredictable, especially with regard to how they will affect us personally. At the start of the second part of this book, we explored the characteristics of complex adaptive systems and the implications for leadership of living and working with change. This is not easy and can be very stressful, with consequences for physical and mental health and general well-being, making a critical connection to the well-being quadrant explored in Chapter 5.

We know that young children require strong attachments with significant adults to develop and thrive (Ainsworth and Bowlby, 1991). Without these secure attachments in place, they will find it difficult to make progress, and will experience stress and insecurity when placed in unfamiliar surroundings. Early experience of change is an important preparation for the future, laying a foundation for life. Balancing support and security with new experiences and challenges is important in early years and needs developing throughout childhood and adolescence. However, we should not regard this as providing sufficient preparation for adult life, the inherent implication being that we should be adequately prepared to cope having reached a certain level of maturity.

We need to identify the skills that are required for managing change throughout our lives. Part of this will be the mindset to accept and embrace change, working with it to the advantage of individuals, families, friends, and communities; recognising and accepting those elements over which we have little or limited influence or control; and making informed choices when appropriate and available to us. The pace of change also must be balanced with the well-being of all those affected. This is an essential consideration for all leaders of the future, who have a duty of care to moderate, manage, guide, and support individuals, groups, and communities.

We will all require support, guidance, and understanding in negotiating periods of intense change throughout our lengthening lives. Ensuring children and young people are prepared and know how to learn to make adjustments to what they do, how they do it, and even who they are, will be a critical part of education for a future of change. Similarly, schools working and engaging with parents and carers should expect that children's progress will be affected at times by changes occurring in the home. This raises the question, to which we will return later, of how support can be provided to families by working with partners in the community.

Ainsworth and Bowlby's attachment theory proposes that when we have a secure, loving base to our lives we are better able to change and adapt. Consequently, when there are changes or losses in our personal lives, then we are at our most vulnerable and will find it most difficult to cope. This has implications for communities and individuals, for the well-being of students and families, and for the sustained performance of leaders and all staff.

David Perkins (2014) considers how we decide what to include in the curriculum in order to prepare children for the future and offers two tests – whether something is *life-worthy* and whether it helps to make children more *life-ready*. Life-worthy learning is learning that is likely to matter to the lives of the learners, so knowledge is only important if we continue to use it. Perkins suggests that the content of the curriculum should be built around those things that are likely to come up again in the future and will help to develop thinking. He argues that, in a world of change and uncertainty, 'general capabilities take on special power – for instance, skills of communication, collaboration, problem solving, and learning' (Perkins, 2014: 23). His vision for learning as preparation for life in a

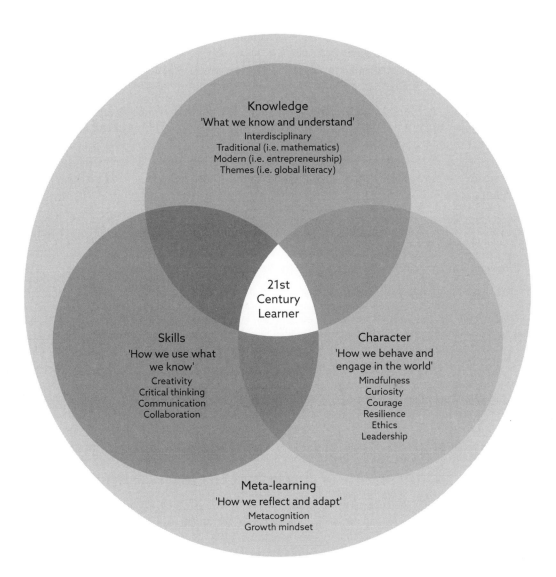

Figure 7: Model of four-dimensional education (Centre for Curriculum Redesign, 2015)

complex and rapidly changing world emphasises how this will need to create independent learners skilled in problem-solving and collaboration (Perkins, 2014: 23).

Bernie Trilling and Charles Fadel (2009) also tackle the question of how best to educate children and young people for the challenges of the twenty-first century. Drawing on extensive research undertaken in the United States, they highlight 'the importance of student-centredness in learning, the value of authentic projects, student interests, relationships and pathways to success, and the globally connected nature of their learning' (Trilling and Fadel, 2009: xvii).

Trilling and Fadel's work is useful in the way that it breaks skills down into different groups and subsets that can be applied in all subjects and contexts. It also provides a research-informed basis for practice, drawing on what has been tried and found effective, whilst providing examples of different approaches in varying contexts. In their more recent work, Fadel, Bialik and Trilling (2015) develop this thinking to identify the 'competencies learners need to succeed' in the future within four dimensions (see Figure 7):

1   Knowledge – What we know and understand.

2   Skills – How we use them.

3   Character – How we behave and engage in the world.

4   Meta-learning – How we reflect and adapt.

It should be stressed that this is not a rerun of the old, and to some extent sterile, traditional versus progressive polarisation of knowledge versus skills. Both must be taught in a curriculum. For example, it is not possible to teach scientific knowledge properly without also teaching understanding of the scientific method, which is, at root, to question all knowledge, even, or perhaps especially, firmly held knowledge. Once we embrace a conception of learning composed of these interconnected dimensions, then an arid debate about knowledge versus skills is completely redundant.

Change study 3: A NICER curriculum

The change that happened at Victoria Park Academy is grounded in a creative view of teaching and learning, and in a curriculum to support that learning which connects directly with the world beyond school. According to Andrew Morrish:

> There's one thing I hope you'll never see at Victoria Park and that is whole class teaching. It's fine, of course, in very short bursts, especially at the start of a new concept, but by and large it has no place in the school.

Central to this thinking is the idea of repeatedly entering a 'learning pit', a term borrowed from the work of James Nottingham (2009). Each episode essentially consists of two main phases of learning – confusion and clarity, depending on whether learners are at the bottom or top of the pit respectively. Pupils are often thrown into the pit with very little support, in the knowledge that they must work collaboratively to get themselves out of it. For example, more able pupils may be thrown in the pit right at the start of the lesson, often with a talking postcard or tablet device with pre-recorded instructions from the teacher. Throughout the lesson, pupils evaluate whereabouts they are in the pit, be it stuck right at the bottom or almost on the verge of climbing out. Conflict is inevitable, but by working collaboratively a solution, and way out, can always be found. Pupils appreciate the independence and challenge as they use their learning tools – for example, their trowel (for revising) or torch (for noticing) – to help them overcome problems (see Claxton, 2002). At its most basic level, getting out of the pit requires only one thing – intelligence, or the strategies you use when you don't know what to do.

In the nursery, children typically plot on a 'challenge-ometer' how difficult they think their task is. The teacher then increases the level of challenge accordingly. If a child wants to draw a flower, the teacher may get the child to include several of the new shapes they learned about the previous day in their drawing, thus making links with real life experiences and with prior learning. As Andrew says:

> Pupils know that it is only when they get themselves out of the pit that they have learned something new and achieved the learning intention. So getting stuck in the pit is essential as it is at this point that new learning takes place. Teachers therefore have to ensure they plan activities which ensure every pupil becomes stuck at some point during a lesson, so they can become un-stuck without support from the teacher.

For such teaching and learning to happen, the curriculum must support creativity and thinking. After many failed attempts and false starts, in summer 2012 Victoria Park finally created its unique NICER© curriculum. Taking inspiration from the Latin origins of the word 'curriculum' (meaning 'running, flowing, lively, eager, swift') this is a bespoke challenge-based learning journey designed to enrich and enthuse all pupils. The NICER curriculum is constructed around the five components of now, independence, creativity, enterprise, and local region. Including each of these five elements ensures that learning experiences are based on children's own interests, with a clear local and regional flavour. All this is carefully mapped and recorded. In Andrew Morrish's words:

> We created a spiral curriculum, by which I mean one that pursues a winding course around a fixed point in a constantly changing series of planes. With all these elements in place, we felt that we had a fit-for-purpose product that met the needs of all our pupils.

At Victoria Park, they begin by asking five central questions about each of the curriculum's five component parts (as shown in Figure 8). From the answers, the curriculum is created around a series of cross-curricular themes, each with an open-ended learning challenge. Skills ladders are then produced for each area of learning, including for each of the 17 learning capacities, derived from Building Learning Power (Claxton, 2002). Claxton groups these capacities around four themes: resilience (e.g. noticing and absorbing), resourcefulness (e.g. imagining and reasoning), reflectiveness (e.g. planning and revising), and reciprocity (e.g. listening and collaboration).

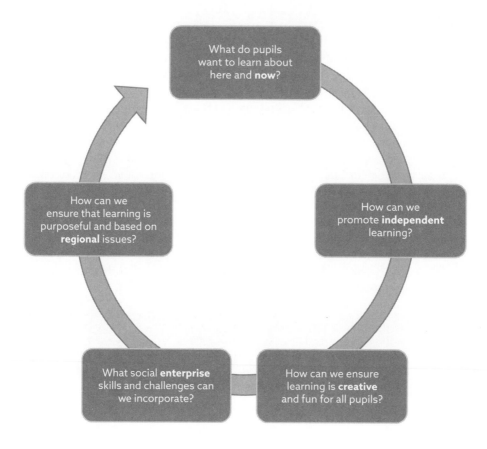

Figure 8: The questions underpinning the NICER curriculum

Many of these cross-curricular themes are based around a social enterprise challenge, such as running a school business, designing an app, or organising a festival, function, or event. Examples of other challenges require the creative use of a range of media including animation, dance, and drama. Nine enterprise skills have been mapped and are recorded by pupils as their learning progresses.

At one level the impact of this change is seen in the school's journey from special measures to truly standing out. But for Andrew Morrish, what is probably even more significant is the learning culture that has grown up and its long-term impact on teachers and learners:

> Being an outstanding teacher doesn't necessarily mean having to teach outstanding lessons day in, day out. That wouldn't be possible and is likely to result in burnout by the end of the first term. Instead, an outstanding teacher should aim to ensure that over the course of the year, every lesson that is planned and delivered is a good one, packed with opportunities for

pupils to be resilient and resourceful, which will lead to learners who are quick to celebrate the fact that if they are stuck, then they are on the brink of learning something new. These pupils (and teachers) will seize the moment and reflect on their new learning, keen to replicate it elsewhere. These are the pupils that truly stand out. These are the learners of today and leaders of tomorrow.

Identity and person-ability

So what is it that lies behind, and might contribute to, building pupils' ability to stand out?

In today's increasingly complex world, knowing or deciding who we are is an important and complicated question that affects both how we see and feel about ourselves personally and how we interact with other people throughout our lives. Our identities are initially presented to us by the circumstances of our birth and then largely shaped by our experiences, but as we grow and develop a wide range of other factors can come into play. If our initial experiences are limited and insular, this is likely to inhibit both the development of our personal sense of identity and how successfully we can interact with those who are different to us.

We can approach identity formation as a creative experience, in which we recognise the differences, sometimes subtle, in how we behave and how we perceive and present ourselves in different circumstances – an awareness we might have from an early age. Negotiating this throughout childhood and adolescence has been characterised as a difficult phase of life for many years. The more complex world we live in – and increased human longevity – means that it is now not just a phase, but a lifelong experience. For example, what is the impact on identity of children having serial parent figures, moving from rural to urban living, changing employment frequently, or living in or with different cultures?

The cultures of localities and schools have always had an impact on children and young people's developing sense of identity. Arguably, too little consideration has been given to the impact of this up until now. Some, perhaps many, have held the view that one of the roles of schools is to help to shape personal identity as part of 'character formation'. We suggest that one of the key roles of schools, in terms of preparation for the future, is to help children and young people to *define* and *create* their own identities. They need to develop the personal skills required to confidently present themselves and interact with others in the range of situations they are likely to encounter on a global scale.

Students themselves will be asking many questions about what they see and experience, including about the implications for them personally. To ignore this is to undervalue them as individuals and to fail to help them prepare for their future. Finally, whilst the current focus on grit, resilience, and character is an essential component, the process is incomplete if we do not consider these qualities in the wider context of identity development. Otherwise we risk continuing to predetermine what individuals 'should be' rather than helping them to develop the skills to decide and adapt.

Emotional literacy

Related to the development of identity and what we have termed person-ability (by which we mean the ability to be confident and strong in who you are and in your own sense of identity) is the emotional literacy, or emotional intelligence, of children and young people. The term 'emotional intelligence' is frequently attributed to Daniel Goleman (1995) following the publication of his successful book of the same name. Emotional intelligence is usually defined as 'the ability to monitor one's own and other people's emotions, to discriminate between different feelings and label them appropriately, and to use emotional information to guide thinking and behaviour' (Colman, 2009: 248).

In the interconnected world of today, where constant change is the norm, emotional intelligence is a more essential quality than ever if individuals are to live happy and successful lives. Acquiring, practising, and refining the qualities of emotional intelligence should not be left to chance – nor should it be assumed that they will be absorbed from experience – but rather should be planned for by the school within the curriculum and formal learning and extended through extracurricular opportunities. Employers repeatedly stress the value of emotional intelligence for employability and yet its part within the curriculum and records of student attainment is very often marginal. Emotional intelligence has, then, a critical connection to both well-being and employability and is probably best viewed as part of the holistic development of the individual.

Values, ethics, and choice

Life in the twenty-first century offers far more diversity and range of opportunities for many, though by no means all, individuals than had been available to previous generations. We have considered how people, arguably, have more freedom to make decisions about their identity and who they are. But in and throughout each day, people have more choices available, and hence make many more decisions. Often these 'decisions' will be in relation to something everyday, mundane, and trivial – for instance, choosing which of the 35 different varieties of olive oil the supermarket stocks to buy or which coffee to order – or they will be taken with little conscious consideration, to comply with norms and to 'fit in' with the expectations of others. As such, a person may hardly be aware that they are taking decisions or making choices on a day-to-day basis, and pay little or no attention to the implications or consequences.

However, a future-aware education makes children conscious, from an early age, of when they are making a decision, the basis on which they are taking it, and its wider implications and possible consequences. Once we become more aware of the decisions we are taking, and their implications, the complexity of the values and ethical choices to apply (or fail to apply) will also become more evident. These values pertain to every aspect of decision-making. The three wide-ranging examples that follow illustrate this complexity and how it extends into every aspect of life. Given this, it is important that all aspects of the curriculum should explore the ethical questions that are raised and facilitate the safe debate of contemporary issues; issues that are frequently very controversial and sometimes supported on either side by powerful pressure groups and interests.

Firstly, in close personal relationships, we often have questions asked of us about our personal honesty. Children are told from a very early age that it is always important to 'tell the truth', but they are also likely to experience situations in which they see others not being completely honest. They may discover that if they try to 'hide' certain things, they can avoid other problems and difficulties. They learn that being open and honest is, perhaps, not always the best course of action or the 'required' behaviour. Such considerations also relate to our right to privacy and right not to tell everyone everything all of the time. The moral complexity of such concepts applies throughout life and will affect the personal and professional lives of us all. Individual integrity is learned at an early age and requires constant attention to be developed and maintained.

Secondly, in a world in which the dominant economic system gives a financial value to everything, and where personal 'worth' is measured in possessions, everyone experiences pressure to constantly consume. 'I shop, therefore I am' might have been said originally as a satirical comment on our consumer culture and society, but its poignancy lies in the fact that for some it can become a philosophy for life. How many people consider shopping as one of their main leisure activities? Seeing value in our relationships with others and in ourselves as people, rather than in the continual acquisition of goods and possessions, is essential if increased rights and opportunities for individuals are not to become synonymous with greed and self-interest. Throughout history, moral education, including identifying what it is important to value, has been one of the main concerns of social and religious institutions. It is a mistake for secular schools to ignore this and not give it similar critical attention.

Thirdly, scientific and technological advances continue to raise questions about what use to make of our rapidly increasing knowledge and skills. Just because we are able to do something does not mean that we should do it, or be allowed to, regardless of the wider implications. Such ethical questions are perhaps most difficult in medicine, as individuals could be fundamentally changed through the manipulation of embryos or genetic structure – perhaps allowing them to avoid certain heritable diseases or develop desired traits. In more colloquial terms, should humans be allowed to play god? Should we keep people alive if technology enables us to do so, or should individuals be allowed to choose the circumstances of their lives and deaths? Our own views are affected by our personal interests and experiences, but increased human longevity will mean that very few people will not be affected by medical ethics questions.

Yuval Harari (2016: 319) considers the implications for the future of humankind in a twenty-first century world dominated by 'the powers of biotechnology and computer algorithms'. He describes a future in which the main products will be 'bodies, brains and minds' and in which there will be a 'gap between those who know how to engineer bodies and brains and those who do not'. If such a doomsday scenario is not to become the reality, as reflected in other aspects of the growing inequities both in the UK and globally, then we must consider how lifelong education can continuously explore and debate how technological and medical advances benefit only some people and what, if anything, should be done in response.

Living a happy, healthy, fulfilled, and safe long life in the twenty-first century will require the ability to make decisions in every aspect of life, taking account of the implications for self, family, and friends, and the wider environment and society. A strong set of values and a clear sense of personal morality and ethics are, in our view, needed to do this successfully, raising the question of how well education provides this in western societies that are largely secular, though this is not to suggest that religions do not have an important part to play in many people's lives and in global society.

In a complex world, there is something attractive and seductive about any narrative that removes complexity, provides answers, and offers certainty. However, such belief systems can become dangerous if they offer an isolated haven away from the real world, or promote a fundamentalist and extremist philosophy that defines others as an 'evil' to be destroyed. We are all more vulnerable to being influenced by extremist views if we have not continuously questioned and challenged what we value and consider 'right' and acceptable in our own and others' behaviour. Moral education is of more importance now than ever before, and we will all have to confront the inherent complexity and choices of the modern world in our daily reality as part of the ethical questions facing society.

Agency

Our final key component for education and learning in the twenty-first century is agency in all aspects of learning and in how people choose to live. If pupils are viewed as passive receptacles to be filled with knowledge and trained in the 'right way' to do things, then we will not only be failing them but potentially even damaging them by not preparing them for the world today and for the future. Agency involves having the energy, drive, and passion to want to do things and to make a difference. It involves inquisitiveness, curiosity, and the ability to collaborate creatively, together with the willingness to learn from mistakes and the persistence to try again to achieve objectives. It applies in every aspect of life – personal relationships, learning, the environment, where we live, the communities we live in, in civic life and in political decisions about our neighbourhoods, country, and international relations. Individuals need to be confident and sensitive in what they do and be able to question and challenge what others do in relation to them. We also need to be more aware of how data from our commercial interactions is collected, stored, and used, with implications for our personal profiles.

The main way in which schools can prepare children and young people to understand how they are perceived by others is through the development of agency in learning – a core skill for twenty-first century life. Arguably, once young people have acquired this agency as a strong mindset then it will be evident in everything they do and the way in which they do it. It is evident in schools with a strong learning culture (not to be confused, necessarily, with schools that achieve high levels of attainment in public examinations) that everyone (students and staff) demonstrates agency in their learning in various ways. Students are able to personalise their own learning and are involved in assessing the quality of teaching and learning, and provide constructive feedback to teachers based on their lesson observations. Students and staff carry out research into different aspects of learning and make recommendations for improvements based on their findings. Students assess their progress and are involved in determining their next learning objectives. Students present and contribute their own findings and understandings to others, including parents and the wider community.

All five leaders of our case study schools have programmes to involve their students as leaders and agents of change, and see this as a way of contributing both to the life of the schools and to the experiences of the students themselves. Helen Holman comments:

> Students have brought an energy that you never get from adults. They see the change agenda perfectly and they understand it fully ... It is having an enormous effect. This, I believe, is where the school will be transformed. You will have student leadership in the classroom and beyond the school as well.

It is not just the school that might be transformed. One of Helen's students, for example, sees they are making a wider difference:

> What annoyed me was a lot of the people who go on about this school being rubbish have never actually been here, so they don't know what it's like. I wanted to make some changes and work with the community so people can see that, yes, this school does have problems, but it's not as bad as people think. I think it's working. We've got much higher opinions of ourselves. Students are taken to account in the community. Down the hill last year, everyone used to throw apples to cause trouble, but now we've been there and spread the word to students, it's not been as bad, and our police community support officer has come and helped us on that.

Students we spoke to were clear that they too had been changed through their leadership experiences:

> I'm not afraid to say that I wasn't the easiest person to have in a classroom when I was younger. But through the leadership work I've done it's given me a second chance and let people look at me twice and realise I'm not that person. I've really changed a lot since I joined this school and I think that's down to them, the way my character has been built up.

The evidence from our schools suggests a possibly significant reciprocal relationship between the development of genuine student leadership – with its dual characteristics of agency for change and community engagement, as opposed to more common, simpler interpretations of student voice – and the wider growth of trust and engagement in a school. Overall, in developing this further dimension of trust and engagement based on student leadership, our case study schools have found:

- The strongest impact occurred where there were clear roles and a focus on leadership development and coaching for the students involved.
- The fostering of genuine student leadership requires support, skills, and judgement from teachers, which are different in nature from that normally associated with classroom teaching.
- Students involved reported that they had developed a range of skills, including in confidence, presentation, and working with people. They also developed an understanding of decision-making and group processes.

The case study schools are beginning to demonstrate that it is possible to involve students from across a wide age range, not just the oldest, and from a variety of backgrounds. However, the experience so far has often been limited to select groups of students as extending this to include all, or the majority of, students remains a significant challenge. The fact that our schools may be involved in something distinctive, which is worthy of further investigation, was best captured by a new assistant head teacher at one of the schools. Speaking to us eight weeks after her arrival from a leadership post in another school, which was designated outstanding by Ofsted, she said:

> In other schools, I've had student leadership in the sense of giving them responsibility, but I realise now (after being here) it was mostly operational not strategic. The guidance we were giving was on an operations basis, not about them thinking, modelling, challenging, doing ... actually being leaders. So I wonder whether some schools think they're doing it, whereas in reality they're just directing, task-orientated. (Groves, 2013: 137)

Change study 4: Students as agents of change

The learning ambassadors at Pershore High School are a group of around 30 students from different year groups. They have been developed and trained to make observations of lessons to help teachers improve the quality of learning. As part of this observational work they decided to identify the level of challenge that occurs in classrooms. This was to follow on from and complement their own classroom experience.

A survey was designed to establish how challenged students felt in lessons. Around 50% of Key Stage 3 students completed the survey. One main finding was that over 22% of students surveyed did not feel sufficiently challenged in lessons, whilst 71% said that the level of challenge was 'just right'. If so many students were suggesting that the level of challenge was 'just right', the learning ambassadors wanted to establish whether they could be stretched further in certain lessons.

Another interesting finding was that 91% of students surveyed suggested that they would prefer to be in classes with peers of the same ability. Whilst students are streamed by ability in some subjects at Key Stage 3, it is not possible for this to occur across the school. This may indicate that not enough differentiation was occurring in lessons and, as a result, some students were not suitably challenged.

Students commonly reported that work needed to be more specifically targeted to their needs in certain lessons. This could include differentiation for those who already understood the work and therefore required a greater level of challenge. Additionally, gifted and talented students required work that would progress their learning more quickly. Furthermore, appropriate work needed to be set for individuals who did not understand or were currently working at a lower level, particularly in mixed-ability groups. Overall, the survey indicated that students were not consistently challenged in all their lessons, which obviously affected the amount of progress that they could make and ultimately impacted on the school's results in the longer term.

This survey did not, however, indicate the specific lessons in which students were not feeling challenged: something the learning ambassadors wanted to understand. For this reason, a second survey, which allowed students to highlight the lessons in which they did not feel challenged, was conducted the next year. This survey covered the same cohort of students – who were now in Year 9 and 10 as opposed to Year 8 and 9. It was decided to use the students who had completed the original survey for consistency, rather than surveying the new Key Stage 3 students. This approach generated information across two key stages, and, particularly at Key Stage 4, there may be less likelihood that answers were based simply on whether the students liked the subject because of their greater maturity. Furthermore, there was a greater number of student responses and so a greater chance of reliability.

Although almost 13% of students indicated that they did not feel sufficiently challenged in lessons – nearly 10% lower than in the previous survey – 82% of students indicated that they felt the lessons were 'just right' – an increase of 11%. The learning ambassadors felt that these results could indicate the possibility of students being stretched further still to enhance progress. An overwhelming 90% of students indicated that the level of challenge varied across different lessons. At Key Stage 4, students highlighted English (24%), maths (14%), and PE (19%) as the subjects in which they felt the least challenge in lessons. Similar to the first survey, 90% of students indicated that they would prefer to be in streamed, not mixed-ability, classes. This is not always possible due to staffing numbers and class sizes. Therefore it was important that staff differentiate work to ensure that all students make progress.

The study clearly indicated that a significant proportion of the students surveyed did not feel sufficiently challenged in certain lessons. In the first survey, 71% indicated that the level of challenge was 'just right', rising to 82% in the second survey. The learning ambassadors inferred from this that students could actually be stretched further. If we add together the responses for 'not challenged' and 'just right', this gives roughly 93% of students in the first survey – and 95% in the second – who said that they were not being challenged enough. Although this makes an assumption, the learning ambassadors believed that strategies needed to be put in place to address the level of challenge in lessons, with English, maths, and PE being the main subjects of focus.

Taking things forward

As head teacher, Clive Corbett agreed to share these findings with the SLT, governors, and relevant heads of department. Strategies were developed to ensure that departments acted upon the findings by providing greater differentiation and opportunities to stretch students. In addition, the learning ambassadors agreed to continue to dig below the surface to find out how certain students, especially those who had suggested they were being challenged, were performing in relation to their targets.

Once the results were taken to the SLT and then on to the school improvement group (comprised of heads of department), it was agreed, in light of their discussions, that challenge should be a key theme in future lesson observations, learning walks, and work scrutiny exercises. The issue was also presented to the governors' school improvement committee, with challenge being a key focus in the teaching and learning element of the school development plan.

Conclusion

Throughout this book we have emphasised that the future is uncertain, changing, and unknown. Because of this complex unpredictability, we maintain that the role of the educator has never been so essential and important. Every aspect of the learning experience of students should be designed to reflect and prepare the learner for an as yet uncertain future; to develop, practise, and refine their learning skills, and help them acquire the ability to learn how to learn. Aspects of this include the social and emotional competencies required to work collaboratively with others in varied contexts and to persevere when the challenges are great and the problems appear insurmountable. The most effective educational organisations are those that embed learning within their culture and consider everyone to be a learner – with the personal responsibility to aspire to improve their learning and to support others.

Preparation for the future is based upon learning how to do things, not just acquiring knowledge about them. Individual and collective agency is a fundamental requirement of a happy, successful, and healthy life, and should increasingly be reflected in the way that schools design and deliver the curriculum, work with families, and engage with other community partners. Such building of social capital helps to develop a stronger culture of high aspirations, improving quality, collaboration, and continuous creative learning for innovation and improvement.

Questions for reflection and discussion

- How is the learning culture of your school defined and consistently reinforced?
- How do students describe the social and emotional skills that they are aiming to develop?
- How effectively do you equip students to be agents of transformation in your school? What about in your community?
- In what ways are students helped and supported to define and develop their personal identities?
- What opportunities are provided for students to talk about what is important to them and to have their feelings recognised?

Chapter 7

The Family and Community Engagement Quadrant

What do we mean by parental engagement? What do we want from it? We know it must focus on learning and support outcomes for students. But if we look at it just from a professional viewpoint, we only see the tip of the iceberg. We need to understand the complexity, not just interpret with professional eyes. We're always trying to put things into a neat box. We need to use a completely different model. I need to understand my parents, my community, more.

Helen Holman

Getting parents involved in the life of the school is not what makes a difference to pupils' learning; the goal is getting parents more involved in the learning of their children. This can most certainly happen in school – but it can also happen in the home (where it will make the most difference; after all, that is where young people spend 75% of their time), in the car, in the supermarket. We need to shift the focus away from the school, and toward the wider sphere in which young people move and live.

Janet Goodall (2014: 17)

Developing a language for engagement

The language that we use to describe the relationship between schools, families, and communities can be very informative about our attitudes and how we perceive the role of schools. Examples of frequently heard phrases include: 'the school at the heart of the community', 'parental involvement', 'the school as a safe haven', 'home–school links', 'parent assistants or volunteers', and 'parental support'. In all such phrases, and you can probably think of many more, the school is seen as the centre, which parents are expected to support as peripheral participants. The emphasis in such perspectives is that it is the role of the school to educate the child and the role of the parent to support the school. Such school-centric perspectives are in danger of presenting teachers as elite professionals who know best, whilst parents should come to the school to learn what they should be doing – and, better still, to help as volunteers, to raise money, to become 'more involved'.

The consumer model that emphasises parental choice has not been helpful in altering this school-centric perception, as it does not actually invite parents to contribute to what is provided by the school. Their agency lies in choosing between predetermined options, rather than in active participation. Their ultimate alternative would be choosing another school, which for many is not an available or realistic option.

So we have to ask: engagement in what? What do parents want to be involved in? Alternatively, from the perspective of the school: if the role of schools is to promote the learning, progress, and achievement of students as whole people, how do they engage with parents and carers to do this holistically?

Desforges and Abouchaar (2003: 4) describe how research consistently shows that 'parental involvement in the form of "at-home good parenting" has a significant positive effect on children's achievement and adjustment even after all other factors shaping school attainment have been taken out of the equation'. In their report, 'good parenting' includes:

- The provision of a secure and stable environment.
- Intellectual stimulation.
- Parent–child discussion.
- Good models of constructive social and educational values.
- High aspirations relating to personal fulfilment and good citizenship.
- Contact with schools to share information.
- Participation in school events.
- Participation in the work of the school.
- Participation in school governance.

Furthermore, Harris and Goodall (2007: 68) suggest that parents need to be seen by schools as integral to learning, and need to know that they matter in this way. Therefore, schools need to provide guidance and support to enable that engagement to happen, with the home as the focus, not the school.

When Helen Holman became head teacher of Orchard School she quickly came to realise that it was in fact the school that was 'hard to reach' for parents and the community. As this was the case, then contacting and engaging with parents would be virtually impossible until the school itself changed. Schools often talk about hard-to-reach families, but how many fail to recognise that the real problem might be that they are a hard-to-reach school?

Helen recognised that, to begin to make progress, everyone in the school needed to understand their families and communities much better. They needed to develop a better and deeper understanding of the local context in which they were working. There is a critical connection here with the other three quadrants of the Schools of Tomorrow Framework, as knowing and understanding more about the main factors within each domain is essential. Complex adaptive systems are dependent upon a constant flow of information and feedback and this comes from involving more people and from the relationships between them. Initially, of course, this can feel very threatening and uncomfortable, but once common cause and purpose is established then the outcomes will be transformational.

Community and communities

Where we come from arguably plays a major part in who we are and how we define our identity. But very few localities are unaffected by globalisation, and the connectivity of the internet and social media means that location need no longer constrain the networks and communities to which we belong. As a result, the terms community, communities, and networks have become less precise and frequently ambiguous. Yet they remain important, if not essential, to us, both socially and emotionally. The social nature and cohesion of the communities and society in which we live are very important factors in providing us with a sense of safety, security, and well-being.

It is difficult to envisage the homes and neighbourhoods in the towns and cities of the future as being radically different to what exists today, and yet changes can, and do, occur very rapidly for different reasons. Since this affects how we live, personally and directly, key aspects of learning and education for the future should relate to our understanding of the places in which we live and communities of which we choose to be a part. This should include an understanding of the environment, the design and construction of our physical world, the social cohesion of our communities, and the degree of connectivity and insularity of localities.

Ballot Street Spice (BSS) is one example of how schools can truly engage with the local community. It originated with Victoria Park Primary Academy's Spice Academy, a weekly after-school spice club which enables pupils and families from diverse backgrounds to come together to learn, cook, and share spice blends. The club has grown into something far more wide reaching than this: BSS is now a full-scale social enterprise.

As well as fulfilling the key ambitions of the school's NICER curriculum, BSS aims to bridge across elements of the local community that it serves. Spice has an evocative social history and is wonderfully symbolic of different traditions, tastes, and cultures. Since the 1950s, people have been arriving in Smethwick from around the world, creating a diverse tapestry of many languages, religions, and cultures. By celebrating diversity and cherishing old traditions, the club aims to bring people together through spice and share their spice stories before they are lost.

BSS seeks to make a difference to the community of Smethwick, whilst making great spice blends and celebrating spice heritage. Profits from sales are reinvested into the company to allow it to do this. It provides employment and learning opportunities for community members of Smethwick who have found it hard to get back to work, or have little or no work experience, and at the same time provides pupils from the academy and surrounding schools with real opportunities for learning – meaning young people can learn about enterprise and develop real life skills, as well as building their confidence.

Such approaches are still relatively rare in schools. However, this type of project can contribute to children's growing awareness and give them the enterprise skills required to ensure that, wherever they are, they can live a rich and fulfilling life connected to the rest of the world. In order to develop this, we suggest that schools focus on four key elements of study:

1   *A sense of place* – This draws on the history and character of the past, but utilises the changing nature of the globalised world of the twenty-first century to creatively define and structure the locality in ways that are equitable and provide opportunities to all who live, work, and visit there. A sense of place will also include an understanding of the local ecology and environment. Global warming and its effects are an issue throughout the world, so it is essential that people understand and appreciate what is happening to the environment in their area and how they contribute to this. The unique character of different areas is to be treasured, but not in ways that resist or inhibit change. Equally, change that tramples over the feelings of different groups of people will result in tensions and potentially segregation.

2   *A place in the world* – Localities that are insular and isolate themselves from the wider world might appear to be havens to which to retreat, but ultimately will not be able to thrive and provide opportunities for those who live there. Outward-looking communities that develop many diverse connections throughout the world, both formal and informal, are likely to have a sense of the contribution they make to the world at large and encourage people to participate in a welcoming community. If learning does not have a global perspective, engagement may be inhibited and limited, even from an early age.

3   *A sense of community* – This is both hard to define and contentious within the context of the growing cultural diversity that has resulted from historical and continuing migration patterns. Community cohesion can appear easier to achieve in areas where most people share a dominant cultural background or where other cultures are in small minorities. In such contexts, people may become isolated if they do not integrate into the prevailing culture, at least to some degree. However, in areas where there is a diversity of cultures, then community cohesion must be created between them, and so takes on a different meaning.

Without meaningful cohesion, segregation can be evident in housing, shops, and social facilities and can extend to other areas of social and civic life. It is important to note that community cohesion is not only affected by culture and ethnicity, but also by the social class, gender, and age of its members. Growing inequalities, in the UK and globally, mean an increased risk that separation will lead to segregation in many localities, affecting cohesiveness. Schools have a role to play in bringing children and young people together in their learning, and in extending this into the communities to which they belong, both within the locality and beyond.

4   *Connecting with others* – The ability to connect is an essential interpersonal, social, and learning skill for being happy and successful in personal relationships, indeed in all aspects of life, and is arguably more complex now than ever before. The ways in which we connect are going to continue to change, and are likely to become more complex as social media extends into new and different fields, perhaps involving the use of wearable or implanted technology. Meanwhile,

the internet continues to provide access to information, ideas, and other people instantaneously, anywhere in the world. Given this, our educational experiences need to enable us to develop a range of skills, including the ability to extend and adapt existing communicative and interpersonal skills in response to changing situations and circumstances. Whether in face-to-face interactions or virtually via social media and the internet, children and young people need the ability to make new contacts and relate with people from different backgrounds. They will need to develop purposeful communication skills and, where appropriate, establish relationships that can be extended. They also need to be able to keep themselves safe from predatory individuals, threats to personal identity and security, and dangerous ideologies. Navigating the various benefits and risks of connectivity, whilst remaining relaxed and open rather than inhibited and overly wary, requires high levels of skill, confidence, and resilience.

These four elements are interconnected, with each mutually supportive of the others. Those who come from and belong to communities that are both diverse and strongly cohesive, that have a strong sense of place and of where they fit within the world, will find themselves in a social and cultural context that supports and encourages their personal connectivity. It should go without saying that there will be negative consequences for individuals and communities if any of these elements are weak or missing. Whilst those who develop a strong sense of their own individuality may have personal attributes that bring some success, their relationships and ability to communicate with a wide range of different people in diverse situations may be limited. Refugees and migrants who experience displacement from their homeland also have to adapt to unfamiliar contexts and develop a new sense of identity as part of the communication and presentation skills required for successful relocation to a new life.

Communities in which personal agency is the cultural norm invite and encourage engagement. These communities also build high levels of social capital. A significant contributor to the inequities within the UK today, which evidence suggests are increasing, is that some communities have more social capital than others (Social Mobility Commission, 2017). This limits social mobility and ensures that those with greater social privilege can ensure that their relatives and social networks preserve their position. If education is to play a more extensive role in countering inequity then schools must begin to contribute towards improving social capital, particularly in those communities and localities where it is currently limited or even declining. This can be achieved, as the example of Roseto demonstrated, by communities working together collectively to build local organisations that raise aspirations and promote social and cultural values to the benefit of the wider community and individuals. School leaders can exercise an important role by working with leaders within the community to establish a range of local organisations that are working towards a common purpose.

Change study 5: Lowering the drawbridge

When Helen Holman came to the newly rebuilt and rebranded Orchard School towards the end of 2006, she found: 'a castle, with a very wide, deep moat, and a drawbridge, and that drawbridge didn't go down very often, and only for a select few'.

Two local schools had recently been closed, with the students from those schools moving to Orchard's predecessor school, causing turbulence across the school community. Reputation and results were not strong. In response:

> I think the school battened down its hatches. I understand in stormy times it's quite a good thing to do in some areas, but it makes you vulnerable to not seeing what's happening out there. There was absolutely no link with any primary school or any other establishment, and this bunker mentality had actually been deliberately fostered.

In this rapidly changing school community, Helen set out to fill in the moat:

> We looked for support from as many people as we could. We started being less defensive and tried to be more engaging.

But it was not straightforward. Helen believed it was necessary to address internal matters before the school could have the confidence or capacity to look outwards too much:

> Community engagement for me hasn't been an easy journey because I've had to get things right here before we could engage with the community. I would have loved to be doing this work sooner, but we just didn't have the capacity. We had to get our own house straight before we could have any kind of meaningful dialogue with key stakeholders.

In Helen's view, engagement does not just mean talking to people, but a two-way dialogue with stakeholders, resulting in shared vision and values between the school and overlapping stakeholders. Her rationale for engagement is clear. The students are her highest priority:

> The most important people I am accountable to are the children in the school. If we don't have the ambition that all our children can be successful, can achieve their potential and more, then we shouldn't be here.

Success for students, importantly, includes a range of elements connected with personal and social development, particularly around communication and confidence, as well as academic achievement. Helen says:

> I want our children to understand that adults aren't an unknown quantity. Too many of my children don't have regular conversations with adults. I want children at this school to be able to communicate and articulate with the different groups within their local community. I also want my children to understand that they have a part to play, that they don't stand as isolated teenagers. Ever since I've been in education I've been struck by how people who aren't in education are very nervous about teenagers. If you say you teach in a secondary school, people

go, 'My goodness, what an awkward age group.' They're not an awkward age group, they're just teenagers, just like we were. I want to help my children understand that they can be really powerful in shaping their own futures, well, shaping their now as well as shaping their futures.

A key element in her strategy looked beyond the individual and the school, towards a joined-up view of education across all sectors and at working differently with parents. Helen describes her vision:

I have this picture in my head. We've brought about internal school improvement, we haven't finished yet, but it's a bit like building a tower. To build it any taller, we have to put some stabilisers out, and those stabilisers are our work with the community. I believe in engaging parents more, and one of our chosen routes to that is working more closely with primary schools.

Helen Howard became Helen Holman's key agent in bringing about this vision. She was previously the local extended services coordinator, but Orchard School took on funding her post part-time when resourcing for extended services ceased as a result of government cutbacks. Her prime task initially was to support the local cluster of schools. Under her guidance this started to develop towards a more purposeful partnership:

The work of the cluster was basically a casual meeting of heads to think about how they needed to work better together and just have some time to say, 'This has happened to me, any advice or help?' or whatever. A number of schools were starting to say, 'Well, actually we have the same challenges, we really have the same families, we have the same community, so we really need to work a lot more closely together.'

Helen Howard has worked to help Orchard School to build a partnership with three local primary schools and children's centres to create this vision of:

separate schools and settings, but with a one-ness about them to make it easier for us to work with our community and to serve our community, so we can work with whole families rather than just individual students whilst they are with us, to help smooth the learning journey for the child from the children's centre all the way through.

They called this partnership With One Voice. There was a steering group, comprising the head teachers and governor representatives from each of the settings. The stated aim of their work was to see the communities they all shared having improved aspirations, for the whole community and for their children:

If we achieved that, everything else would be falling into place. People within school might verbalise it slightly differently, because in school it's very much about attainment and results, but if we had aspiration, then attainment and results would really improve dramatically. You've real issues around here in parents engaging in their child's education and having any idea that it is at all important, or beautiful, or helpful.

For Helen Holman:

> I think we do understand that engaging with our community is the way we can establish the ground we've made, make it good in terms of the outcomes for students that we've already achieved, and improve on that. I want the school, the students, the parents, the stakeholders to feel confident in this school. I think a confident school builds a confident community, and a confident community builds a confident school. We have to start with the confident school because our community isn't a confident one at the moment.

Helen Howard's role was gradually extended to include the development of student leadership and the formation of a parent council. Capacity was created through a combination of opportunism and risk-taking. She was joined by a marketing manager to help change prospective parents' perceptions of the school – an ex-governor who was also formerly the deputy editor of the local paper, and began to work more closely with the recently appointed school transition coordinator, whose role was to work with local primary schools on all transition issues, including progression and continuity.

The partnership schools agreed to share the funding for Helen Howard's post, and together they set about organising a succession of programmes and events, beginning with a successful community fun day attended by about 400 people. The group then grew in confidence and began working towards more complex and focused activity. One such initiative is a long-term strategy developed with health and community partners called Staying Alive. This is designed to tackle the high rate of mortality in the community and address the issues of obesity and life expectancy, both for children and parents. The intention is to create a spiral curriculum – starting with the Year 7 science, PSHE (personal, social, health, and economic education), and ICT curricula, but then eventually rolling down into all primary schools and back up again throughout Key Stage 3 and 4 – with long-term impact for both children and parents. Partners involved in the programme include the local council, through the use of their fitness facilities, and community nurses. In addition, a farmers' market is held on the Orchard School site to help address nutrition. Helen Howard says:

> It's in our hands. We must be brave. People don't want the message. But if we can't do it, who can?

Increasing parental engagement has been a challenge at Orchard School. Attempts to engage more than small numbers in a formal parent council have stuttered. As Helen Holman puts it:

> We know what fourteen reachable parents who come to meetings want. More homework, better reporting, more communication. But they're not necessarily representative. My other parents don't feel it's relevant to them.

She had realised that parents are not one homogeneous group, but come from many different backgrounds and each has their own views. There was a need to think about what was distinctive for each of them. It meant turning things on their head a bit, perhaps stopping to listen rather than telling parents what the school wanted:

> We try to work alongside and enable, but who are we to say what that work should look like, that our parents need to know more about maths or literacy to help children? We're still stuck in a circle of thinking we know what parents want.

Helen Holman's conclusion is indeed radical, and whilst the pace has sometimes seemed slow, the results have also been unexpected:

> I want to throw everything out – you start to grow something and you don't know what it's going to be, a bit like free knitting, if there is such a thing. We can do that now. I'm feeling more comfortable about the messiness of growth; things are in place now that make that approach more viable. I'm not an expert. I've been battling with community engagement for a long time. We've not achieved half of what we thought, but I've perhaps modified what I thought to achieve. It's been a slower journey, even though I'm impatient for change. But maybe this has begun a movement. We measure impact in ways I hadn't expected, and perhaps I've had to modify what I thought we could achieve. When I started, I was about raising the profile of the school as a positive learning community, increasing pupil numbers, being a better school. We've done those things. But it's actually about much more than this.

Change has not happened as a result of one thing or a sequence of things. Growth is not linear. Rather, it has been about getting the conditions right in a number of areas and letting change grow. Helen Holman is beginning to see important evidence of change:

> I sometimes think we only ever change one thing, but then we're also waiting for other aspects to be at the right stage for the next development. There's not a direct one-on-one relationship between what we do and the result. It's not a matter of 'do this and it causes that to happen'. We've made our boundaries more fluid. We were isolated from our community, with low self-esteem. Now we're proud. Our self-esteem has increased as a school, for children and, increasingly, parents. We were a hard-to-reach school, and to an extent we still are, but we're changing. We've prepared the ground to do that work now. The confidence of parents and the community has changed to allow us to do that.

Conclusion

Learning is changing. Through technological advances it is becoming more accessible and more open to personalisation. This means that schools will eventually have to adapt to new contexts of learning if they are not to face increasing challenge from students, families, and communities who think that schooling does not adequately meet their requirements or is irrelevant.

That implies school leaders and staff need a much deeper understanding of what parents and families think, and how to work with them, for increased engagement in learning to happen. To really engage parents and community members, staff must be prepared to listen to their views as the basis for further discussions and to find a common purpose, recognising that initially this may be uncomfortable and difficult. But only genuine family and community engagement in learning can be the basis for building meaningful learning cultures in communities.

Questions for reflection and discussion

- What language around family and community engagement is used within your school? Does this consistently reflect the values of the school?
- How would you describe the family and community context of your school, including with regard to engagement in learning?
- How does your school contribute to developing the social capital of families and the wider community?
- How can families and your school work together more effectively to increase engagement in learning?

Conclusion to Part Two

To some extent it has been an arbitrary decision on our part to link which change studies to which quadrant. That is because of their mutually reinforcing nature. There is not a series of linear, sequential steps to find a way of putting them into practice. Of course, each of these second-horizon leaders found a starting point for their school, but they were very quickly operating in multiple ways, some big, some small, to bring the quadrants to life in the experience of the school and its pupils.

Each of our leaders sought to build a deeper, shared understanding of school purpose and quality, one which they believed would better equip the young people in their charge to live successfully in a world of future change, whilst also meeting necessary governmental and societal demands in the present. In each case, the leadership of the head teacher has been a critical factor in making such change both possible and successful. In Part Three we try to understand further the nature of that leadership, what makes it distinctive and different, and what the wider system might learn from it. Developing more such leaders will be the most crucial element in meeting the demands of tomorrow today.

Questions for reflection and discussion

- In what ways has your view of the four quadrants changed through your reading of Part Two?
- How has your view of the second horizon developed as a result?
- What strikes you most about the five leaders and their varying approaches to the leadership of change?

Part Three:
Leading for
Tomorrow Today

Introduction:
Simply Complex

A defining element in our understanding of change lies in a growing appreciation of the significance of complexity thinking. This involves understanding a school, and the environments to which it relates, as a complex adaptive organism rather than in terms of the more linear and predictable organisation of, say, a machine or factory. Through this thinking we can glean a better understanding of the processes of change and thus of long-term improvement for the schools of tomorrow.

In contrast to linear, hierarchical assumptions about change, where strategies are imposed from the top, using a complexity mindset permits a different way of contemplating intervention. Complexity thinking requires a move from a linear to an organic understanding of change, drawing on the three associated concepts highlighted in Part Two: emergence, connectedness and feedback.

The concept of emergence implies that, given a sufficient degree of complexity in a particular environment, new, and to some extent unexpected, properties and behaviours will emerge. New properties and behaviours emerge not only from the elements that constitute a system, but also from the myriad connections between them, which multiply exponentially when the scale is right. The part played by positive feedback is crucial in this process. Whilst the circumstances that give rise to feedback may have been random, self-reinforcement leads to lock-in of a particular phenomenon through a process of autocatalysis – that is, where the product of the reaction is itself the catalyst for that reaction.

All these concepts from complexity theory, we have argued, have some resonance in illuminating the work of our five leaders. This conceptual understanding may therefore be able to help us shape the foundations for a more organic and holistic theory of school change and system leadership than the current paradigm of school improvement allows. At the heart of this paradigm lies the belief that it is most effective for a school to focus all its energy on what is under its direct control and influence. This has led to an increasingly exclusive focus on the importance of teaching, and in particular subject knowledge, allied to a single dominant type of assessment.

Our counterargument rests not on the belief that teaching or knowledge are unimportant, but that they are not sufficient on their own to grow confidence, self-esteem, and motivation to learn, to equip students to thrive in a changing world, or to sustain raised aspirations in a challenging environment. These beliefs are derived from a clear foundation of principles and values, and supported by a range of evidence, as Chapter 1 shows, including – importantly but certainly not exclusively – our case studies. The types of improvements we need to strive towards, our case study heads suggest, come most effectively if we address two interconnected dynamics.

The first is a focus that moves beyond, as well as within, the school to include engagement with learners, their families, and communities around common purposes. The second is an understanding of organisational change which is more akin to the model of the growth of a living organism. For example, the human body does not grow the arms and then grow the legs; rather all aspects of the body develop in concert as the individual progresses towards maturity. But for this to happen, certain other developmental conditions – such as having adequate nutrition or reaching a certain age – need to have been met. So the underlying processes of change may be better understood as a series of expanding waves, strengthening in all directions simultaneously, albeit with certain sequences possibly inbuilt.

There is, however, a dilemma inherent in the understanding of change that we are suggesting and which these five leaders have pursued. It is the tension between what we will call transformational change and incremental change.

On the transformation side of this equation lie the examples of the Pony Express, the Cutty Sark, and Wittgenstein's propeller. Each of these innovations were, in their time, examples of the highest performing, fastest, or most efficient technology. However, they were all superseded and rendered effectively obsolete, not by a later model doing the same thing better but because of the introduction of something completely new: namely the railroad, steam power, and the jet engine. On the incremental change and marginal gains side of the equation lies the British Olympic cycling team and successful Formula One motor racing teams, who each improve their performance through the aggregation of many small, specific gains.

Both paradigms of change have a place, but the time, situation, and circumstances need to be right for each. Indeed, many small, incremental shifts can add up to a major transformation. One useful way for those inhabiting the second horizon to bridge these two views lies in another organic model: metamorphosis, a process of change experienced in different ways and to different degrees by many species. A series of small changes occur, imperceptible in real time, which at a certain critical point eventually give rise to a new form or being. Change here may be more or less gradual, and more or less complete. However, for that change to happen to the fullest extent possible for a particular organism, certain developmental conditions – such as nutritional needs and a readiness on the part of the organism to respond to the promptings of growth – need to be met.

Pools or ponds?

One powerful and illuminating image to help us understand this perspective better is provided by Charles Darwin in the final paragraph of *On the Origin of Species*:

> It is interesting to contemplate a tangled bank, clothed with many plants of many kinds, with birds singing on the bushes, with various insects flitting about, and with worms crawling through the damp earth, and to reflect that these elaborately constructed forms, so different

from each other, and dependent on each other in so complex a manner, have all been produced by laws acting around us. (Darwin, 2006 [1859]: 388)

The world is very complex, made up of multiple interactions and unpredictable variations that lead to an almost unimaginable range of permutations. This is not remote science but rather a way of understanding the world in which we live. Quite properly and understandably we aspire to simplify the complexity of our lives, but in doing so we may well misunderstand the forces controlling certain aspects. We want the world to be rational, predictable, and manageable, but therein lies the rationalistic fallacy. The world is not as neat and predictable as rational planning models would have us believe. Equally, any attempt to simplify the world might compromise the richness of alternative futures.

Think of a pond next to Darwin's tangled bank. It is not managed, it changes with the seasons, and as some life forms grow, others die. It is essentially a complex adaptive system – the result of a wide range of variables interacting in a way that is understandable but not replicable. Now think of your local swimming pool, deliberately and systematically managed so that, whilst it is safe, it is also sterile and un-evolving. Leadership surely means coming to terms with the complexity of the pond and its tangled bank rather than seeking to control a school as we would manage the pool. We can seek to understand, but we may not be able to predict patterns of change. We can foster the conditions for growth, but not necessarily control them. The pool is essentially a product of managerial perspectives – of limited first-horizon thinking that functions within narrow and reductionist criteria and is primarily concerned with the effective maintenance of an essentially sterile environment. Second-horizon thinking would encourage us to explore alternative ways of managing the pool as well as developing alternative futures.

In this final part, we examine the nature of this change of perspective and the implications for leadership. In Chapter 8 we distil from the experiences of our five leaders and their schools six defining characteristics of change leadership. Then, in Chapter 9, we tease out what might be learned from applying our understanding of these characteristics at two different levels – the leadership of school improvement and the development of system leadership. In the final chapter we return to the ancient wisdom which posits that effective leadership of oneself is the precursor of effective leadership of others, and think about what this might mean today for ourselves and for our schools. Finally, in a concluding postscript, we take a peek over the third horizon at what might one day, given our values and our commitment, emerge from the tangled bank if our leadership can positively nurture the conditions for growth, manage the present creatively, and engage our communities well along the way.

Questions for reflection and discussion

- To what extent do you see your school as a pond or a pool?
- In what ways is this reflected in your leadership?

Chapter 8

Understanding and Leading Change: Six Defining Characteristics of Leadership for Tomorrow

What marks out our five leaders is that they have begun to think differently about school improvement, and therefore about change and themselves as leaders of change. Our five are certainly not the only leaders we could have chosen to study, as many are no doubt questioning existing models and thinking differently. This chapter is an attempt to further understand the nature of that difference.

We will do this by considering six striking features of their leadership of change, evident in the change studies and in their interviews. These six stand-out and, importantly, interconnected features are:

1 A clear sense of values and personal authenticity.

2 A commitment to fostering quality relationships.

3 An understanding of complexity allied to a deep sensitivity to context.

4 A commitment to meaningful collaboration.

5 A focus on building community capacity.

6 A loose–tight leadership balance which combines empowerment and agency with clear values, a shared purpose, and joint accountability.

Firstly, however, it is worth addressing a rather basic question.

Why change?

We have argued throughout this book that creating the school of tomorrow involves change. Such change has to be seen as emergent rather than as an event. However, change is not always self-legitimating and in some contexts may actually be seen as part of the problem rather than a possible solution. Some may feel that a moratorium on change would be the most appropriate response to many of the challenges we have identified. We would respond by arguing that change is inevitable and is embedded in every aspect of our personal and professional lives. Change is the norm.

We argue strongly that this means we need to start to reconceptualise how we perceive every dimension of life in schools in order to respond to the imperative to rethink and innovate all aspects of education, not least regarding the role and nature of leadership. But, because change is not a self-legitimating process, it is necessary to offer a rationale. This can be based on permutations of the following propositions:

- Current strategies are not working and may in fact be counterproductive, so there is a situation of diminishing returns in which increased investment is being matched by declining outcomes.

- More effective and efficient means of working have been identified – as with the move from propeller to jet engine discussed previously. The purpose remains the same but the means change out of all recognition.

- There is a need for the organisation to model its core purpose in its roles and structures. For example, if the core purpose of a school is high quality learning, and learning is perceived as being primarily a change process, then the school should exemplify a learning community.

- Change may be required in response to authoritative evidence, such as the EEF Teaching and Learning Toolkit, referred to in Chapter 1.

- Change may be non-negotiable as a result of directives in government policy or contractual obligations.

Each of these five justifications for change forms part of the basis of the work our five leaders have undertaken. Taken together their experiences point to the inevitability of change in order to secure the schools of tomorrow. This work is most often encapsulated in their use of the four-quadrant framework, and their understanding of the interdependence and interaction of each quadrant. In practice, how have they approached this change process and what has made that process both possible and successful? This question led us to examine what we think are six distinctive characteristics of their leadership.

1. Leading change through clear values and personal authenticity

My values are about doing the best possible job for children and their families, with a belief that, however fractured the education system is and however much government tinkers, it's incumbent on us to step up and do the right thing for children.

I hope what I do is be very transparent. I took over in my first headship from a respected head teacher, but one who was very paternalistic. I need people's ideas to be shared with me, so I think out loud, ask people. I don't think I have to be the one person who has to have the answer to everything. Leadership is an extension of my teaching career. When you're a teacher, you have to inspire, you have to get people to think, coach them when needed, mentor when they're getting it right, give them words of hope when they're getting it wrong. You give them wings to fly, and just a few key questions when they're going off track. I see leadership as an extension of this.

Julie Taylor

A clear sense of values and personal authenticity is the first of our six leadership characteristics. In several cases this has been forged through our leaders' own formative experiences of education, including the commitment of their own parents who, because of personal experience of disadvantage, wanted to ensure their children had the opportunities of which they had been deprived.

For example, this is Clive Corbett's story:

It comes directly from my background. My background wasn't poor but it was a humble background. As a child, with my sister, we were brought up in what would now be called social housing, in council accommodation. If we were subject to the current measures we would have been pupil premium. I was fortunate enough to have a mother and father who believed passionately in the importance of education. When my dad left school – this was in the mid to late 1940s – he came home with a letter from his headmaster saying that he had gotten him a job as a trainee reporter on the local paper, *The Express and Star*, in Wolverhampton. And the letter was proudly waiting for his father to open when he got back from the coal mine, and he looked at it and crumpled it and threw it into the fire telling my dad that he'd got him a proper job at the drop forge in the iron works, and that was just the way things were then. That then drove my father and my mother. She'd always felt that she was not good enough to mix in certain company. My dad had this passion to get ahead. He got out of the forge, moved to the Post Office, got through to some pretty significant clerical jobs, including postmaster. He escaped, though without the formal qualifications, and he was therefore determined that I would escape from that background.

Julie Taylor has a not dissimilar story to tell:

I think there are things I've had instilled in me by my upbringing, an ordinary working class upbringing. My parents both had to leave school at 14 because of poverty, even though my father had won a scholarship to Manchester Grammar School. Being forced by his parents to leave at 14 and take what he thought was a very boring job with financial security, he was determined for me and my brother that we would have choices. They didn't have choices. My mum's father died when she was 10, so she had to go out and earn money. She wanted us to have choices about what we did with our lives. And that's really what drives me. It is the same principle for all children. Some young people are born more equal than others; they come to school with more advantages, not always obvious ones. And it's about just trying to offer every young person that comes to school a sense of belonging, a sense of knowing they can achieve and get things right, knowing that everyone makes mistakes, but knowing also that they can achieve, and helping them put it back together when it goes wrong. I have a passionate hatred of the 'Look what's happened to me' culture of the media which has glorified being a victim, where people say, 'Woe is me, I can't do this because of what's happened.' I absolutely detest this part of British culture. I think there's a responsibility on education to enable every young person to cope with whatever life throws at them. Everyone's got a backstory, everyone has had something happen to them, and it's how you face both triumph and adversity that matters.

Clear values and personal authenticity resulting from inner conviction are central to any model of effective leadership, particularly when engaging in any sort of change process. To change people's values and beliefs – or, perhaps better, to persuade them to change themselves – involves both integrity and authenticity. The process is rooted in strong values, respect, and a commitment to people and to giving all children a chance, though not at the expense of staff. Indeed, it is worth advancing the hypothesis that the potential success of any change initiative is highly correlated with the values and authenticity of the leader.

In practical terms values and authenticity might be expressed in the following ways:

- The ability to articulate, explain, and justify personal values.
- The moral confidence to apply values in practice without compromise.
- Transparency and honesty in all dealings.
- Morally consistent behaviours – fairness.
- Personal and professional credibility – 'walking the talk'.
- Openness and integrity – being visible and accessible.
- Sustained commitment and engagement.

2. Leading change through quality relationships

In our school, it is the welcoming nature, to anyone who comes in, that is important. They can stay, they can just observe, they can be part of us for as long or as little as they want. So that could be parents who are settling in their children. We don't have a set format for settling in. We have a personalised approach for every child and every family, within a framework of our values and what we believe in, and I think that's what makes our community. But equally we are very open to change and to having that genuine feedback from parents about what they want from us, because everyone wants something different. I think that is what you can observe when you come, because I don't know where else in the community you would see that.

Isabel Davis

In the final analysis, learning is a social process. High quality and successful learning requires high quality and successful relationships. Any model of learning or change has to incorporate the relational dimension as a highly significant variable. Learning and change are both more likely to succeed given the extent to which relationships are seen as a pivotal criterion for success.

It is easy to forget the very wide range of emotional responses to change. For some change is exhilarating, for others it is intimidating and deeply disturbing. Overcoming very real concerns and anxieties, however motivated, is one of the key elements of the successful leadership of change.

There are virtually no aspects of effective leadership that do not require high quality and sophisticated interpersonal relationships. At the very least, leaders have a responsibility to acknowledge the centrality of the relational dimension in securing deep and embedded change. However, trust is also about the very simple day-to-day working relationships that make the difference between a school that is an authentic community and an organisation that is based on hierarchy, control, and micromanagement.

It can be argued with some confidence that trust is the key performance multiplier that enables the full range of leadership activities to happen, for example:

- Leading innovation and change.
- Creating an interdependent supportive community.
- Developing confidence between parents and the school.
- Developing confidence between learners and teachers.
- Working with marginalised groups and families.
- Supporting school improvement.
- Building learning relationships.
- Enabling creativity and risk-taking learning.
- Enhancing personal well-being.
- Creating high performing teams.

3. Leading change through an understanding of complexity allied to a deep sensitivity to context

This journey has got a vision, but we're having to modify as we go along. You try something and it doesn't work. It's a bit like evolution, sometimes appearing haphazard. But we're not just changing as result of chance or external pressure, but because of reflection on our journey and learning. The work to increase social capital in our community and help it to be confident is imperative for the school's success.

Helen Holman

Leaders of second-horizon schools have to be confident and comfortable in two respects that are not part of the historical canon of school leadership: understanding of complexity and sensitivity to the influence of context. Complexity has already been discussed at some length, suffice it to stress here that leaders have to be confident and at ease whilst working in a period of significant relativity in which historical certainties are no longer available. The period since 1997 (beginning with the advent of New Labour) has seen the reconceptualisation of education in England, with a range of historical certainties being challenged – such as the legal status and funding of schools, the nature of the curriculum, and the models of assessment and accountability.

Alongside this dimension of complexity is the importance of recognising the significance of context – particularly with regard to the nature of leadership and the ways in which schools are organised. As English society becomes more diverse and polarised, so schools need to be sensitive and responsive to their contexts.

An understanding of complexity and sensitivity to context would seem to have the following components:

- Contextual intelligence – mapping the real and the virtual worlds.
- The ability to analyse and synthesise complex issues and relationships.
- Gathering evidence from multiple sources.
- An intellectual openness combined with humility.
- The ability to explain and secure understanding in order to engage others.

4. Leading change through collaboration

In forming our MAT, our discussion has been about an inclusive ethos; this is the core of the vision statement we've come up with. It states the MAT is a family of schools striving to work collaboratively and forge strong links with parents and the community to encourage and promote respect, responsibility, and a lifelong love of learning within caring, compassionate, and stimulating environments. We aim to inspire our pupils though an engaging and exciting curriculum, whereby they will be well prepared for all stages of their education – from age 3 through to 19 – and to achieve their full potential; to become positive, confident, and active members of the local community and global society of tomorrow.

Clive Corbett

For many people life can be a balancing act between the desire for social interaction and the need for personal autonomy. This is often reflected in how organisations function. Some choose to actively seek integration and collaboration, others follow a more solitary path. The tension between autonomy and collaboration is a very real issue – it is manifested in every playground and every staffroom. In some ways autonomy is perceived as strength and collaboration as symptomatic of relative weakness.

Schools are often classic examples of this tension. On the one hand there is a very powerful tradition of autonomy, often derived from the focus on institutional accountability and the need to compete for pupils as the market-based culture has become increasingly significant in education. On the other hand there is often recognition that, professionally, there is a need to be open, to share, and to collaborate in order to secure the best possible outcomes for pupils. This has not always been the case – there have been times when collaboration has been important for its own sake and it has not resulted in sustained progress in pupil outcomes or significant, consistent school improvement. Another issue is that if, as is frequently asserted, schools have a duty to prepare young people for the world of work, then schools should model the level of collaboration that is often found in working environments.

What is clear is that in terms of schools for the future, whilst the need for autonomy is understandable, in fact the need to collaborate is the greater imperative – however challenging and counterintuitive it might appear to be. The gradual movement into the various permutations of MATs and other forms of partnership point to a very different working pattern for many schools in which collaboration is the organisational norm. This in turn implies rethinking certain long-cherished assumptions about school leadership.

Leadership for change involves the development of a collaborative culture with most of the following characteristics:

- The ability to develop a moral consensus.
- Skills in reconciling competing priorities.
- The willingness to be open and work collaboratively.
- Skills in negotiation, bargaining, and compromise.
- Building relationships through networking.
- Managing projects to turn plans into practice.

5. Leading change by building community capacity

> We spent a lot of time building a shared federation, a shared community of learning across the three schools, focusing on reducing variations, improving consistency. But now we are at the point where we need to redevelop our uniqueness. Each school has always been unique. We needed to come together as three communities and now it is time to go back and look at ourselves as unique communities. Obviously, the people and the environment set the tone within that community. They are the weather of that community, and that changes. It is not just people who are in school; it is people in the actual, physical community, whether it is faith leaders, or our parents or grandparents, or people who have an interest in us – stakeholders, governors.
>
> **Isabel Davis**

The leadership of change in schools can lead to two highly dysfunctional outcomes. Firstly, the complexity of the change process, and sometimes the lack of skill and experience in leading change, can result in senior staff acting unilaterally to save time and get things done. There are times when this is appropriate and necessary. But it is not for the long term and it is not for sustainable deep-rooted change. Andrew Morrish (2016: 93) talks from his experience about three stages of change, characterised as tightening up (getting the school out of special measures), loosening up (flooding people with creativity and giving them permission to innovate, including permission to fail), and powering up (embedding the change and building capacity and sustainability). That is when the real transformation happens.

Secondly, the high stakes that can be associated with successful change in terms of influence and power mean that the leadership of change can degenerate into micropolitics on a par with an Italian Renaissance court, where Machiavelli is perhaps the most appropriate guide. The antidote is partly to do with creating a moral consensus, and partly to do with creating a sense of community based on a superordinate sense of shared purpose, using strategies and processes focused on high quality relationships. In simple terms, this implies that the leadership of change should be an activity rooted in community principles and practices.

The chances are that a highly effective school of tomorrow will have most of the characteristics of a community which is high in social capital. In effect, the school functions as a particularly sophisticated community, especially in terms of the quality of relationships. One of the key characteristics of schools as communities is that they focus on the central activity of schools – the various elements of learning. One way of understanding this is to see schools in terms of Wenger's (1998: 253) model of communities of practice, which has much in common with the components of high social capital:

> An organization's ability to deepen and renew its learning thus depends on fostering – or at the very least not impeding – the formation, development, and transformation of communities of practice, old and new.

According to Wenger's model, a community of practice shares three elements:

1 A clear sense of mutual purpose and commitment to a common area of social, economic, or occupational activity – examples of such communities might include the members of an allotment society, a specialist surgical team in a hospital, and many forms of teams in education.

2 The development of a strong sense of collaborative working, sophisticated networking, and the sharing of ideas and practices that enable interdependent learning – for example, through social media.

3 A focus on actual practice, which is supported by the development of a shared language, techniques, and strategies.

An effective community of practice will mature and develop through the development of such shared practice. This in turn will build social capital and so develop as a virtuous spiral, with each stage of growth reinforcing the integrity of the community. This can be found in almost any successful high-performing group – success breeds success and social capital breeds community.

> Social capital increases your knowledge – it gives you access to other people's human capital. It expands your networks of influence and opportunity. (Hargreaves and Fullan, 2012: 90)

The leadership agenda for change requires a focus on the development of social capital in order to maximise the potential for engagement in change. In basic terms people are more likely to embrace change if they feel that they are part of a supportive community that shares the commitment to change. Building community capacity therefore involves:

- Securing commitment to shared norms and values.
- Developing rich networks and quality relationships.
- Supporting rich dialogues across the community.
- Creating a sense of shared identity and ownership of place.
- Encouraging shared learning.
- Affirming and celebrating success.

6. A loose–tight leadership balance which combines empowerment and agency with clear values, a shared purpose, and joint accountability

I don't have a single style of leadership now. I style-flex, and use different approaches. Knowing when to use the stick, or the carrot, depends on the stage of the school. I am very affiliative from the outset in a sponsored school. So I give out lots of permissions, and do that really quickly – permission to fail, to innovate, to delegate. I believe you distribute leadership as quickly as you can. And I say, 'I'm out to follow you, walk alongside you, help you.' And I do lots of coaching, though that may be the calm before the storm. I think they have a term to show us what they can do. If there's no improvement, then I'm more pace-setting and coercive.

When I started in headship, I went in with all the expectation of the hero-leader nonsense. It doesn't get you anywhere. It gets a quick fix, but nothing else. So I take a more laid-back approach now, delegate a lot. I trust people – and I expect that back – for instance, keeping me informed if something goes wrong. I'm more confident in doing that now because, when things get difficult, staff themselves are now referring to our values.

Andrew Morrish

At the time of writing there has been a recent surge of interest in leadership styles triggered by Hill et al.'s (2016) article in the *Harvard Business Review*. The research concluded that the prevailing image of successful leadership is actually wrong. On the basis of an extensive survey, which considered a wide range of variables, the researchers were able to relate leadership behaviour and actual impact.

Hill et al. claimed to have identified five types of leaders: surgeons, soldiers, accountants, philosophers, and architects. The surgeons and soldiers actually did more harm than good, with schools eventually worse off after their appointment ended. Yet surgeons were often extraordinarily well rewarded for their failures. Some 38% of the sample had received knighthoods and another 24%

some other honour, such as a CBE. They also received payment which was typically 50% higher than the average for a head.

Heads classified as accountants did improve the financial position of their schools. Whilst this is an important factor, their leadership made no measurable impression on exam results. Philosophers were popular with their fellow teachers. They spoke the same language and appreciated their workforce. Again, there were no significant improvements during the philosophers' tenure and performance had coasted or declined after they had left.

The fifth and final type of school head, described by the researchers as architects, believed that it took time to improve a school. They therefore took a long-term view of what they needed to do. Amongst other things, they improved student behaviour by moving poorly behaved students into a separate pathway, increased revenue by developing non-teaching offerings, and improved teaching and leadership by introducing coaching, mentoring, and development programmes. Examination results typically started improving in the third year of their tenure and continued improving long after they had left.

The reality, however, evidenced by our five leaders, is that there is no single model for successful leadership. All displayed elements of each style, and none at times, although all were committed to long-term sustainable impact. Yukl (1999: 302) rightly observed:

> Vague definitions of leader 'types' have long been popular in the literature, but they are often simplistic stereotypes with limited utility for increasing our understanding of effective leadership.

Most of our five leaders have undertaken an assessment of their emotional intelligence, analysed against fifteen characteristics, based on the model developed by Bar-On (2006). What became clear was that there was no single pattern and often quite significant differences between the leaders. The one characteristic which showed the strongest agreement was their self-awareness, and that is perhaps entirely unsurprising. They are acutely aware of themselves and of the people around them, and can choose how to relate and interact effectively to achieve their goals.

Fullan (2015: 10) noted:

> Top-down change doesn't work because it fails to garner ownership, commitment, or even clarity about the nature of the reform. Bottom-up change, so-called 'let a thousand flowers bloom', does not produce success on any scale. A thousand flowers do not bloom and those that do are not perennial.

The implication of this, as demonstrated by the evidence from our five leaders' schools, is that a balance between loose and tight provides an optimum leadership style. That does not mean there is a single 'right' balance. It will shift according to context and time. Getting the balance and timing right is the role of leadership, and a significant factor in the success of our five leaders. In this, acute self-awareness is one major ingredient. Enabling leadership encourages empowerment and agency amongst staff – trusting them to make the right decisions at the right time – but does so within a clear framework of shared values, a common purpose, and joint accountability.

To enable valid and sustainable change, leadership styles should arguably incorporate elements of the following:

- Being fit for purpose in the sense of being sensitive to the culture of the school and to its context in terms of performance.
- Balancing control and trust (loose–tight relationships) as is appropriate but looking to increase trust.
- Moving from managing to leading – i.e. focusing on the strategic.
- Building leadership capacity by sharing/distributing leadership.
- Explicit and rigorous accountability.
- Robust and challenging review and analysis of leadership effectiveness.

Conclusion

Of course, these six characteristics are not a linear sequence in practice. They interrelate, interconnect, and reinforce each other. They do not come from a manual or textbook, but from a deep sense of values and purpose. Underpinning all the characteristics lies a sense of authenticity in terms of identity and relationships – at both a personal and an organisational level – and a sense of agency and empowerment. Leadership may be the crucial enabler for this, but its effects are mediated through others and are highly dependent on context.

To a great extent, the leadership practice we have observed and described, rooted particularly in the experience of these five successful leaders, runs counter to much prevailing orthodoxy, which pushes towards centralisation, control, and rigid predetermined outcomes. There is some way to go before this experience will be sufficient to enable us to understand the nature and appreciate the effects of such a shift. In the next chapter, though, we will try to distil from their leadership practice what we believe is an emerging picture and around it seek to make some critical connections.

Questions for reflection and discussion

- How do you weigh your own leadership of change against each of the six characteristics identified here?
- Are there elements you would want to develop further now? How might you do that?
- Are there any significant features of change leadership which, in your view, are missing from this analysis?

Chapter 9
Connected Leadership: Two Areas of Focus for Thinking Differently about School Improvement

Working from the insights into the nature and leadership of change that we have outlined, one of our starting points is to suggest that existing models of school improvement have significant limitations. It is not so much that current improvement goals are wrong as that they are insufficient on their own, and inherently self-defeating if pursued in isolation. The reason for this is partly demonstrated by the growing critique of the statistical basis by which school effectiveness has come to be judged, as argued by Gorard (2009), for example, and cited in the introduction to Part One. Yet the data this generates still forms the basis underpinning most school improvement thinking.

To understand what Gorard means, perhaps consider this extract from a blog by one leading head teacher:

> Getting ready for the term ahead, I've been analysing my school's RAISEOnline and, after I suspend disbelief and start working within the (slightly bonkers) framework of convoluted algorithms, it's a complicated story. Some areas are Green; some are White and one or two are Blue. Our figures for Disadvantaged Pupils are strong – mostly Green. Despite being well below national average on raw overall outcomes, the cohort was 70% disadvantaged with a low entry profile and VA [value added] is very strong. You see, it's a complex picture. I'm starting to think about the likely inspection this term and our SEF [school self-evaluation form] and I'm not sure what line to take. We'll probably go for 'Good'. It's a 'best fit'. But what's that about? Why should we need to find a best fit? Why can't we tell our complicated story? Who benefits from reducing it all to a one-word descriptor? I can't think of a good reason to do it. (Sherrington, 2014)

But Gorard, as we also noted in Part One, relates this substantial statistical problem to a wider, deeper criticism of current models for school effectiveness which unwittingly encourage an emphasis on assessment and test scores – and teaching to the test.

Inadequate goals give rise to limitations in understanding of methods. This in turn can lead to:

- An over-focus on teaching at the expense of learning.
- A focus on subject knowledge, with insufficient emphasis on the interlinking of learning skills and character development.
- An underappreciation of the relevance of both context and engagement.

- An overemphasis on a consumerist model of schooling at the expense of a shared responsibility for learning across schools, families, and communities.

An explanation as to why current thinking about school improvement can only take us so far is perhaps most starkly captured in this significant comment made by Moreno et al. (2007: 5), reflecting our analysis in Chapter 1, and with broadly similar percentages:

> The tragedy of school change is that only about 30 per cent of the explanation for variations in school achievement appears to be attributable to factors in the school.

This returns to a theme highlighted throughout the preceding chapters. The implication is that, if we are serious about far-reaching long-term change in what schools achieve, we must start to think differently both about what that means and how it can be realised.

This chapter is constructed around two closely interconnected foci of change for school leaders who want to live and lead successfully in the second horizon: leadership for school improvement and leadership of the system. The two have become intimately intertwined in English schools in the early part of the twenty-first century, particularly through the advent of MATs as the government's preferred organisational form.

For each of these twin areas of focus, we attempt to explore the implications of our understanding of change in terms of complexity thinking: seeing schools and their communities as complex adaptive organisms. We will consider what this perspective might mean for the next stage of school improvement. Finally, we will explore a concept of connected leadership which has grown out of reflection on what we have been hearing, observing, and thinking in the course of our research. At root this means that by locating leadership more broadly – rather than just within the organisation of the school or school system – the dynamics of relationships are shifted, with students and families empowered to take increased responsibility for their learning.

The term 'connected leadership' has been used by others previously, notably Drath and also Hobby et al. For Drath (2003: 3) it means 'more inclusive and collective leadership'. For Hobby et al. (2005: iii–iv) it is 'a model of influence for those without power'. Our understanding of the term includes, but goes beyond, these two insights. With Drath's work we share an understanding of leadership as a process rather than a task, but add a fresh insight into the nature of organisational change. With Hobby et al. we share a model of influence which is both multidimensional and two-way. However, Hobby et al. look purely within the closed environment of a school organisation, and at the interactions between members of that organisation, whereas the model of connected leadership proposed here is also focused on leadership beyond the organisation, albeit for very specific purposes connected with learning.

The model of connected leadership we propose here goes beyond the current concept of 'system leadership' as derived, for example, from the work of Hargreaves (2011), even though there are some similarities – for instance, in the emphasis on the importance of trust and reciprocity. System leadership, as currently understood, has been primarily about the connections between schools, and the ways in which they can support other schools to achieve school-focused ends. By contrast, connected leadership relocates the locus of leadership so it exists between schools, learners, and their families and communities, seeking to act on and cause each to interact differently with the others so as to promote broader and improved learning outcomes.

This model does represent an explicit challenge to the view that schools should only focus on those factors directly within their control, which is reflected in much recent political orthodoxy – emerging in policy terms in 2010 with the then new government's White Paper, *The Importance of Teaching* (Department for Education, 2010). It does not, however, in any way challenge the need for a school to be the best it can be in terms of its core purpose of teaching and learning, as we firmly articulated in Chapter 1.

Rather, our argument is that, on its own, focusing on school-controlled factors can only achieve so much. Such a focus will not be sufficient either to develop fully that broader set of skills and attitudes which will equip young people to flourish in a rapidly changing world, described here in shorthand as 'personal and social development outcomes', or to bring about sustainable change where there are local cultures of educational indifference and low aspiration. Thus, in the model of connected leadership being proposed, the role of the school leader, albeit with a clear and important role within the school, is equally understood to extend in significant ways beyond the school itself and into its wider stakeholder networks.

Focus 1: Connected leadership for school improvement

Drawing on international research, Barber and Mourshed (2007) conclude that without an effective head teacher it is unlikely that a school will have a culture of high expectation or strive for continued improvement. A huge amount of research and thinking has been devoted to understanding models of school leadership in terms of their impact on teaching, learning, and assessment outcomes. However, far less attention has been paid within education to the role of school leadership in creating and sustaining social capital, what sort of leadership that requires, and how leadership can effect change in that area. Indeed, paradoxical though it may seem, arguably more interest has been shown in relation to understanding the link between leadership and social capital in the business world than in education.

Maak (2007), for example, argues that business leaders have to deal with the moral complexity resulting from a multitude of stakeholder claims, and must build enduring and mutually beneficial relationships with all relevant stakeholders. This he terms 'responsible leadership' and its key component is 'the ability to enable and broker sustainable, mutual, beneficial relationships with stakeholders, to create stakeholder goodwill and trust, and ultimately a trusted business in society' (Maak, 2007: 331). The responsible leader 'acts as a weaver of stakeholder relationships and as broker of social capital in pursuit of responsible change' (Maak, 2007: 340).

According to Stone-Johnson (2013: 670), applying this concept in an education context:

> Responsible leadership in practice means weaving in those who have typically only been recipients of leadership to full-fledged participants and developing relationships with them that serve to benefit not only students but also the stakeholders themselves.

Again, from a school perspective, Sergiovanni (1998) proposed the notion of pedagogical leadership as the pre-eminent component, greater in significance than what he terms bureaucratic, visionary, or entrepreneurial leadership, in bringing improvement to schools:

> Pedagogical leadership invests in capacity building by developing social and academic capital for students and intellectual and professional capital for teachers. (Sergiovanni, 1998: 38)

In Sergiovanni's view, community-building is a powerful way for school leaders to develop capital. He argues that the value of capital generated as schools become communities is more important in determining a school's success than are its physical and financial assets. Both the leadership and development of the school as a community, as well as the leadership and development of the school in the community, are, he suggests, necessary – and neglected – parts of school effectiveness. He concludes:

> When students have access to social capital they find the support needed for learning. But when social capital is not available, students generate it for themselves by turning more and more to the student subculture for support. (Sergiovanni, 1998: 39)

The picture we have been building suggests that the next stage of school improvement requires a more complex understanding of the relationships between schools and learners; between schools, families, and communities; and between learners, their families, and communities. It also means paying closer attention than is often currently given to a much wider set of learning outcomes in the personal and social domains – even though we may not be able to measure them as precisely – whilst at the same time scaling back some of the pre-eminence given to external test-based academic outcomes, bringing both into a new and mutually supportive relationship through a more powerful focus on self-worth and a resulting sense of achievement and success. This in turn reflects the belief that, fundamentally, everyone is a learner and has a desire and the ability to learn.

Figure 9 represents a first attempt to understand and represent the interaction between these wider insights, as glimpsed in our five schools, and to begin to theorise and to capture some of this emergent thinking. It suggests that traditional school improvement thinking only addresses half the picture – the shaded area in the top-left half of the diagram. Broadly speaking, this area represents the insights of established thinking on school improvement, focused on the school as a self-contained entity and on the quality of teaching and learning therein. Leadership exerts a major influence on that and on securing recognised attainment outcomes for learners (as shown by the darker central arrows acting outwards on all three domains).

Of course, the great majority of schools also pay some attention to outcomes associated with personal and social development for learners. These are not, however, the prime concern in most cases and usually are only partially addressed. Moreover, parents and students often feel excluded from leadership for school improvement (Foster, 2005).

In contrast, the white triangle (the bottom-right half) represents the area of additional leadership which, if understood and secured, might afford a more complete picture of educational achievement. In this view, students, their families, and communities share significant responsibility for outcomes, not only attainment outcomes in the accepted sense of the term but also those wider personal and social development outcomes which are crucial for the learner, citizen, and worker of tomorrow.

The figure demonstrates that these wider outcomes have an importance in their own right, but in addition can contribute to the achievement of more established attainment outcomes through increased motivation, confidence, and self-esteem. Moreover, those qualities of confidence, self-esteem, and motivation may influence the long-term development of families and communities.

The notion of connected leadership stands at the centre of these two areas of school improvement and wider engagement. It seeks to harness the forces of growth and impact within each and to bring greater alignment between them in order to improve the learning of pupils both within and beyond the school. The role of both trust and engagement is central to developing the conditions for such growth. Connected leadership understands it is nurturing a pond, not managing a pool.

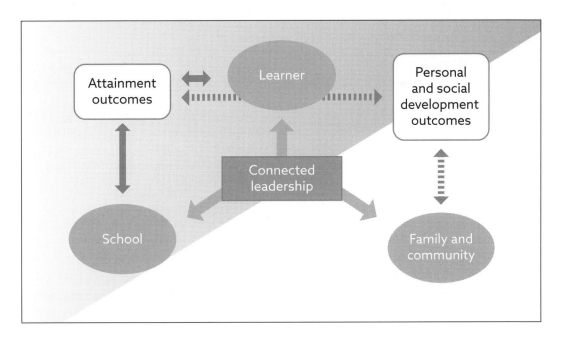

Figure 9: A model of connected school leadership

The leaders of the schools of tomorrow therefore look to engage with families and communities around a broader set of school purposes and outcomes, which – as a side effect – can also contribute to the next stage of raising attainment in the narrower sense. This is because each learner has developed their own motivation and, importantly, also has the confidence of and in their families and communities.

So, in summary, we think there is a case for constructing a new model of school improvement, incorporating the following key features. It would:

- Allow for a central role to be actively played by children and young people, and also their families and communities, in informing judgements about success.
- Recognise complex rather than linear models of change.
- Be developmental rather than compliance-led.
- Recognise the significance of context.
- Be congruent with national expectations, but – through a broader vision of school purpose and quality – move beyond these, rather than adding an additional layer to them.
- Make a distinctive contribution to long-term improvement in terms of its methodology based on a different understanding of change.

In such ways and through such understanding, it may be possible for imaginative and enterprising leaders, operating within the second horizon, to help forge the schools of tomorrow today.

Focus 2: Connected leadership for the wider school system

The school journeying confidently towards tomorrow – which is able, amongst other things, to reimagine and develop new sets of relationships and engagement with its learners, families, and communities – will be the product of a process of growth rooted in collaboration and cooperation. That is the opportunity which exists within the present growth and evolution of MATs, albeit hindered by the threat of a national accountability system which is no longer fit for purpose.

Each of our five leaders is engaged in a wide range of collaborative endeavours. At the time of our research, two were in the process of forming new MATs. In each of these cases, we interviewed leaders in all the partner schools as part of the evidence-gathering process. Another of our five leaders was leading a relatively well-established MAT, and a fourth had been involved in turning a pre-existing group of trust schools into a MAT. The fifth of our leaders had formed a successful hard federation and a teaching school alliance. The relationship of TSAs to MATs is one of the great mysteries of current policy, and leaders on the ground appear to be just trying to find ways to make sense of the policy that work for their context.

The challenge of system development in these times is too complex – and the stakes are too high – for acts of individual social heroism, bureaucratic control, or dogmatic prescription to work.

It requires genuine cross-school structural collaboration, and this is one of the most important insights into the government policy thrust around the growth of MATs. The major problem which this policy faces is to retain the right amount of individual organisational autonomy in each context, whilst ensuring that stakeholders are more than agents or consumers. Any school leader contemplating engaging with MAT development, from any perspective, needs to have very clearly thought through their approach to this issue, because it is very much a statutory one-way street. There is currently no route back once a school is committed to it.

It is important to stress that true cooperation and collaboration is much more than token consultation or partial inclusion. The history of human success is essentially the story of genuine and inclusive collaboration and cooperation. Equally, the history of human failure can usually be attributed to the failure to collaborate. From the earliest hunter-gatherers to the triumphs of civilisations, human progress has been most rapid through collaboration. We are essentially social animals and are at our best (and sometimes our worst) when we are working for mutual benefit:

> This behaviour is instantly recognizable in chimpanzees grooming one other, children building a sandcastle, or men and women laying sandbags against an impending flood. Instantly recognizable, because mutual support is built into the genes of all social animals; they cooperate to accomplish what they can't do alone. (Sennett, 2013: 5)

It is a myth that collaboration and cooperation involve some sort of denial of individuality or can only function in a competition-free environment:

> In this respect swarms in nature have taught us two lessons. The first is that, by working together in smart groups, we too can lessen the impact of uncertainty, complexity and change ...

> The second lesson of smart swarms is that we do not have to surrender our individuality. In nature, good decision-making comes as much from competition as from compromise, from disagreement as much as from consensus. (Miller, 2010: 267–268)

Perversely, the history of education and schooling has tended to go against this idea of collaboration. Teachers have long worked as essentially autonomous professionals, schools have always been highly autonomous institutions, and pupils, their parents, and other stakeholders have been subject to partial or conditional involvement. Indeed, the movement from parental involvement to parental engagement is a very powerful image which reflects the nature of the challenge. Parents are commonly highly engaged with their children. The problems seem to start when school structures, procedures, and norms become involved, and possibly compromise a focus on learning.

The problem with a history and culture focused on autonomy in education is that it means we may lose access to one of the most powerful qualities and strategies available to human beings – collaborative working in the true sense:

> We have to learn not to be too inward looking, petty minded, and competitive. When it comes to the structure of society, for example, we have to step out of the narrow confinement of looking after our relatives or our own kind. (Nowak and Highfield, 2012: 283)

Collaboration and cooperation are deeply rooted in what it means to be human, but that does not mean they are automatic or easy. Matthew Taylor (2013), chief executive of the Royal Society for the Encouragement of the Arts, Manufactures and Commerce (RSA), offers an analysis of successful collaboration derived from social anthropological theory:

- From an individualistic perspective, collaboration must be seen to be in the interests of those engaged.

- From a solidaristic perspective, collaboration needs to be underpinned by trust based on sufficiently shared norms and values.

- From a hierarchical perspective, system and organisation leaders – recognising how hard it is to establish and maintain – have to enable, incentivise and support collaboration.

Taylor argues that, in almost any human context, collaboration will only work if individuals are engaged and motivated, there is trust rooted in shared norms and values, and leadership prioritises collaboration. He then goes on to explore the implications and potential benefits of this broad social analysis for education.

Effective collaboration could enable a step change in the functioning of the school system at six distinct levels:

- Relationships between the centre, localities and schools; which are too often characterised by suspicion, misunderstanding and resentment.

- Relationships between schools; which are rarely as robust and committed as they should be.

- Relationships between teachers; which are too often absent or shallow but could be the foundation for continuously improving professional practice.

- Relationships between schools and other local bodies; which tend to be weak or merely transactional.

- Relationships between teachers, pupils and parents; learning is still too often seen as something that is done to pupils not with them, and parents seen as re-enforcers of the school's requirements of pupils.

- Relationships between pupils; even though team working is vital in the modern workplace, and children can powerfully support each other, we still see schooling primarily as a process of individual endeavour and ranking. (Taylor, 2013)

One way of understanding the importance of collaboration is to see it in terms of problem-solving – people come together to collaborate and cooperate to solve problems. Whether it is the nomadic hunter-gatherer clan working in unison to hunt their next meal, different disciplines within engineering coming together to solve problems encountered in building a bridge, or a group of schools working collaboratively to close the achievement gap across the community, the issue is one of joint, consensual problem-solving. It could be argued that – irrespective of context, culture, or era – people spend most of their lives working with others to solve problems of varying degrees of significance and complexity.

Strauss (2002: 32–33) offers a model of problem-solving that focuses on the process issues, in particular the dynamics of relationships and the centrality of cooperative and collaborative working. For Strauss, collaborative problem-solving needs to be understood using the following principles:

- Problem-solving is heuristic – there is no one best way and it is essentially a process of trial and error.
- Problem-solving goes through stages and may involve recognising the need to adopt an alternative strategy.
- Problem-solving skills can be learned – individuals and groups can develop a repertoire of strategies to help in the problem-solving process.
- Those involved in a collaborative problem situation need a common language, a shared vocabulary, in order to communicate and engage with each other effectively.

Hansen (2009: 44) offers a business perspective on collaboration, its advantages, and disadvantages with the following insights:

- The goal of collaboration is not collaboration itself, but greater results.
- Leaders can achieve higher returns on investment as a result of collaboration.
- Collaboration must focus on improvement in terms of innovation, sales, and customer service.
- Collaborative projects must be cost-effective and designed to make an impact.
- The barriers to collaboration must be addressed.

Success in nature, in business, in community, in health promotion, and in scientific innovation seems to be directly related to collaboration and the ability to cooperate. It does appear to be the case that the greater the focus on innovation and creativity in an organisation, the more it works through collaboration and cooperation, and the less it uses hierarchical or control systems. This in turn implies a very clear sense of purpose and high levels of trust, which consequently enable rich and complex networks and an openness and willingness to share.

What was crucial for each of our heads was building a critical mass of support and engagement in change. Penuel and Riel (2007: 615), drawing on their research in 23 Californian schools, comment that:

> This sort of trust gets built up interaction by interaction, tie by tie, within a school. And at some point, it becomes a characteristic of the network as whole ... No one can say exactly what the threshold is for the emergence of this kind of trust. Even in the best schools, trust is not likely to exist within every relationship.

One of the key challenges of collaboration is that the type of leadership needed to achieve what Lasker et al. (2001) term 'synergy', or effective partnership, is not the most common form of leadership. Writing in the context of health partnerships, they contrast the often narrow range of expertise and the controlling behaviour of traditional leaders with the advantages brought by:

> boundary-spanning leaders who understand and appreciate partners' different perspectives, can bridge their diverse culture, and are comfortable sharing ideas, resources and power. (Lasker et al., 2001: 193)

The leadership style of each of our five heads was a key component in the effectiveness of the partnerships and synergy they were creating. Two common themes recurred in our talks with the five leaders:

1   A belief in a culture of collaboration.

2   A sense of being part of a wider educational whole, not just a single school.

As a result, all five heads had in different ways established their posts with a focus on partnership development. Moreover, all were actively exploring ways to develop some form of all-through schooling in order to reduce the many discontinuities associated with transition.

Implications for MAT development

England, in particular, appears to be moving towards a school system organised primarily around MATs. There are a number of striking characteristics evident in the way our case study leaders have approached the MAT concept and begun to turn it into practice, whilst applying the four propositions from Chapter 1. They have tried to learn lessons from the weaknesses that had been evident in implementation so far, and have also applied the positive lessons from trying to develop connected leadership in their individual schools to this broader canvas.

So far, a basic dichotomy of models has been at the heart of the development of MATs nationally. In some cases, joining a MAT has been akin to being issued with a compulsory purchase order. There has been no choice, and only limited consideration on anyone's part as to the fitness of the match. It is perceived on all sides as a takeover. In some cases, this has involved the wholesale imposition of systems, policies, and practice by the trust's leadership without any recognition of a school or community's context or history. Whilst in the most extreme cases this may be justified by the poor quality of the education pupils are receiving, this should only happen in quite exceptional circumstances.

This approach, or the perception that MAT development will necessarily entail this approach, has created a lot of resentment and apprehension amongst many school leaders. The leaders we have been studying, who are themselves involved in MAT development, have looked to find a new balance between independence and centralisation. Julie Taylor comments:

If I look at some leading academy trusts, one of the things families don't like is having a one-size-fits-all blueprint, so that wherever you go, this is the brand, everything is done in the same way. I don't believe you have to do that. It's like bringing up children in your family. They are each different, and as a parent you can treat them differently because they have different personalities. You apply values and principles which are the same, but the way you do it differs according to their personalities. I believe that about the context of different communities. So you can have the highest aspirations, and try to engage communities really effectively in what you are trying to achieve with them for young people. Make sure every child feels known and valued, give them more than exam results, extracurricular experiences, if you like, which enrich them and enhance their understanding of the world in which they live, give them key skills and strategies to face life, stand up to the unexpected and face challenges. But that doesn't have to be done the same way in every single school in the MAT.

For Andrew Morrish:

How to balance commonality and difference is the biggest challenge in creating a MAT. We now talk about a family of schools – not a trust or a MAT – a family working together in ways that allow us to do things better or differently than we would alone. The focus on family has been helpful to us – defining our different families. It's been like unpacking an onion – children, staff, parents, local communities.

It is striking that both Julie and Andrew, independently, fall back on the image of a family as illustrating the relationships they are seeking to develop within their respective MATs. It is perhaps symptomatic of their deep understanding of the centrality of high quality relationships in the achievement of sustainable change. This pursuit of high quality relationships in turn implies respect for the contribution that each partner can bring to the whole, even if in some areas they may be weaker than in others. Julie notes:

Leadership of a MAT presents challenges. One school works in a way I think is right, but the challenge for me is how to work with other experienced heads in a way which doesn't insult them as professionals or dismiss their leadership style, how to take stock of what they're doing, and how to enhance and apply what they're doing not only to their school but also across the group of heads to benefit the greater good of the whole trust.

Forming high quality relationships takes time. There are stages to go through, akin, in a way, to traditional courtship. It involves testing on both sides, trialling small steps, building on successes, addressing difficulties honestly. There has generally been insufficient recognition of the need for due diligence on the part of schools forming or joining MATs in approaching this as a two-way, not just a one-way, process. For this is a relationship, like marriage, with long-lasting consequences. It involves entering a different legal status and structure, as any school joining a MAT becomes an academy, if not one already; an irreversible process. Furthermore, it involves passing major decision-making power away from an individual school's governing body to a corporate board, a possibly distant and unelected board of directors, and, ultimately, to civil servants, the regional schools commissioners (RSCs).

Central to such due diligence is ensuring commitment in terms of clear shared values, as well as absolute clarity with regard to decision-making, processes, and responsibilities. For Clive Corbett, shared values are the essential starting point:

> We were very careful that the first conversations with other schools were to establish that we had shared values. The values of the Schools of Tomorrow Fellowship are very much what will drive us. It's about the development of the young people, and indeed the staff who work with them, in the broadest sense. It is about ever closer links with parents and the community, because we all agreed in these MAT discussions that within our schools, even though we are pretty fortunate in terms of our intake, there are small but significant pockets of deprivation, both within the town of Pershore and in the outlying villages.

A sense of values has also been central to the development of Andrew Morrish's trust. These were co-developed across all stakeholders and are encapsulated in the Latin word for trust – *fides*. This stands for their five core values:

- Focus on family.
- Insist on excellence.
- Do good as you go.
- Embrace innovation.
- Seize success.

The expectations around these core values are being co-developed by all stakeholder groups, and increasingly form the basis from which the trust measures its progress – an example of measuring what you value not valuing what you measure in practice! The values have also made decision-making regarding the incorporation of new schools into the trust a much more straightforward process.

A second key component, around which due diligence is needed, is structural integrity. For the MATs we investigated this involved, firstly, a strong focus on locality. Schools needed not to be too far apart geographically. Our leaders defined this variously as the distance you could drive in a lunch hour, or no more than 30 minutes.

Secondly, structural integrity involves size. The MATs are all currently on the small side, and are growing, but the leaders share a strong feeling that they should not get too large. Julie Taylor believes it is essential for the CEO to be regularly visible in each school, to be recognised by pupils, and to know, at first-hand, as many people as possible:

> you still have to build relationships and community. It doesn't matter if the organisation is huge – to the people in the organisation, there's only one of you.

However, growth also needs to be carefully planned, with a clear rationale, to secure sufficient capacity and economies of scale to be viable in the longer term.

Thirdly, structural integrity involves building systems and processes for shared decision-making, resource allocation, and quality assurance. Both Julie and Andrew have been developing structures for sharing staff expertise across schools, pooling resources, and achieving economies of scale, whilst securing genuine involvement in decision-making by all partners. For Julie:

> Schools are just like a mixed-ability class – they're at very different stages of their leadership journey. How do I ensure consistency when I'm not at the helm every day? Our driving principle moving forward is: how can you establish an organisation that is so effective that people can be doing things differently depending on context but the overarching principles mean people are values-driven – they make a decision in the same way – it doesn't matter if they do things differently because everyone is doing the right thing for those young people, and every child gets the same chance?

Within all this there is the need to very clearly figure out and develop the roles and understanding of all stakeholders. Clive is looking at it this way:

> We have agreed that obviously with any MAT there has to be various statutory structures of members, directors, and so on. We are going to pop in the middle of this what we might call the 'education achievement board'. That will comprise representatives of each of the schools, and the job of the board will be to ensure that our vision lives in everything that is done. So, on that board there will almost certainly be a representative from each school, there will probably be a primary and a secondary school improvement partner, but above all – and this for me is the exciting bit – there would also be at least a couple of community members who would be able to keep our feet on the ground in terms of the way that the MAT is going forward, so it's remaining true to the community's vision.

Conclusion to Part Three

We remain neutral on the desirability of the growth of MATs. We do not in general believe that structural reform is a magic wand: it is more often a matter of rearranging the deckchairs on the *Titanic*. The potential benefits of reinforcing meaningful collaboration could, however, be worth grasping; although, as all the MATs in our study have recognised, this includes wider collaboration beyond the MAT as well as within it and poses demanding new challenges for leaders. Fundamentally, if any emerging form of system leadership does not apply the principles of connected leadership, we believe a meeting with an iceberg will one day be inevitable.

An understanding of system leadership which remains entirely school-centric and does not seek to engage differently with families and communities will not succeed in effecting the deep, long-term improvement we now need.

Questions for reflection and discussion

- Looking at your own leadership, what is the balance of leading within and beyond the school at the present time?
- On reflection, in what ways would you like to adjust the balance moving forward? How will you achieve those changes?
- What are the implications in terms of your own involvement with the development of MATs or other forms of school-to-school partnership?

Chapter 10

Leading Oneself

If you want to be a leader, you have to be a real human being. You must recognize the true meaning of life before you can become a great leader. You must understand yourself first.

Confucian wisdom (quoted in Senge et al., 2005: 180)

Self-awareness and the weaving of relationships

We hope that your reading and reflection, regardless of how you have approached this book, will have encouraged you to understand the urgency and importance of leading schools within the second horizon. We hope you will have gained a greater insight into the forces driving the future our pupils will be entering and be convinced of the need to better equip them to understand and help shape that world. We hope you will have strengthened your conviction that change is needed and that what we are being asked to do at present as school leaders by government policy is just not good enough.

That it is not good enough, however, is not because of the insufficient effort or commitment of leaders and teachers in schools. Nor is it because of flawed structures, incoherent as they may be, in England particularly. Nor is it a matter of inadequate funding, welcome and necessary as more resources may be. It is not good enough because the system in which school leaders are working is constrained by too limited an understanding of the purposes of schooling and, hence, of what outstanding quality truly looks like. It is not good enough because the focus is too fixed on the present (and the past) and not enough on learning for the future and for life. It is not good enough because too often students are regarded as passive receptacles of knowledge and are not engaged as active learners with their own sense and skills of agency. It is not good enough because students continue to be assessed individually and rewarded for 'getting it right', rather than being encouraged to be creative, innovative, and collaborative and to learn from their mistakes. And it is not good enough because that narrow vision has led us to mistake schools for machines rather than see them as complex adaptive organisms, and, as a result, to pay insufficient attention to the communities within and around them.

We also hope you have increased your confidence in the fact that change is possible; that school leaders can live and lead successfully in today and tomorrow at the same time – building a broader, deeper vision of purpose and quality, whilst addressing and managing the pressures of today. And we hope your resolve to grow a strategy to move your school forward in that direction – from whatever place you are now – has been strengthened, likewise your courage.

The five leaders we have met recognise there is never going to be a completely clean slate on which to start to draw something new. That is why nurturing a process of adaptive change and engaging stakeholders is so fundamental. That is why they all focus on building engagement and modelling and stimulating agency.

A picture of leadership as enacted by our second-horizon school leaders has emerged from our studies, and seems to be capable of addressing both the improvement of school performance and the enhancement of social capital within and beyond the school itself. We have termed this 'connected leadership'. It does not easily fit into any single established leadership model, even if we were to assume that these have any real validity. Understanding the ways in which such leaders consciously and unconsciously adopt, blend, and adapt components of existing leadership models to meet the needs of particular contexts and moments in time may be an important area for further research. The leadership exemplified in our five case studies has, nevertheless, provided some important elements for consideration.

The picture that emerges from our consideration of these five leaders' work is a complex and subtle one. Each has combined flexibility, whilst listening to a range of voices, with conviction and consistency of purpose. They have used judgement and opportunism in choosing and timing their strategies, and understood and accepted risk in doing so. At the heart of change lies the principle that leadership should model the behaviour desired from others: a principle that our leaders have both understood and lived out. They have all established 'loose–tight' structures and encouraged collaborative working at every level, both within and beyond the school.

We have also suggested that effective second-horizon leadership is characterised by strong self-awareness, and is highly emotionally intelligent. It can recognise the inevitability of conflicting interests and the need to continually rebalance these around a sense of common purpose. The power held by the leader can assist this task, and there were situations in which our leaders had no choice but to impose a solution. In such cases, this decision was fundamentally driven by their values rather than the expediency of circumstance.

Resolution of conflict is not just a matter of finding the settlement each party would accept, or the lowest common denominator around which different interests could cohere. It is also about seeking to move each group to a different point in their understanding of the whole. This can, in the process, increase the potential for conflict – and the resulting lack of trust – between the demands and expectations of different stakeholder groups. It is too easy to assume that growth in trust and engagement, fostered by good leadership, removes all tension. There is also an important sense in which an element of tension or conflict can even be a positive factor.

Gordon and Seashore Louis (2009: 25) argue that the development of trust and common purpose amongst school stakeholders has a significant part to play in conflict resolution, and note that this is not a win-lose scenario:

> Schools that are open to parent influence are also open to teacher influence: it is not a 'zero sum' power game, but an expanding pie ... In addition, by discussing possible differences in an open and accepting culture, opportunities for resolution and compromise may be increased.

The goal of engagement cannot be the elimination of conflict across stakeholder expectations, but rather the creation of a climate in which differences can be explored and understood with respect. In this, the role and behaviour of leadership is central. The significance of the behaviour and values of the five leaders has been a recurrent theme in our research. This includes their commitment to openness and transparency, the quality and character of the relationships they forge, their willingness to both challenge and be challenged, their resilience, and their clarity of purpose.

So, any leader who aspires to work in this way needs first to develop their leadership of their own self through fostering and exercising these qualities and attributes. This requires great self-awareness and is reflected, in turn, in the ability to judge what response and action is appropriate to a given context. Acute emotional intelligence, and the ability to foster the growth of these qualities in others in order to build emotionally intelligent teams, means a key part of the leader's role is, as Maak (2007: 331) put it, to be a 'weaver of stakeholder relationships'.

In a real sense this is all equally valid and true whether one is leading on the first, second, or third horizon. So, is there anything distinctive or different we can add about second-horizon leadership and its associated understanding of schools and communities as complex adaptive organisms? We think the answer is yes. There are some essential additional characteristics, evidenced in the various change studies we have presented.

Our second-horizon leaders:

- Are at ease with change, accept it as healthy and normal, and respect organic growth.
- Think holistically and do not fragment.
- Search for and identify critical connections.
- Build a strong culture and clear sense of identity.
- Create flatter and more engaging structures.
- Reinforce patterns of behaviour (fractals) throughout the organisation.
- Encourage creativity and innovation.
- Build engagement at all levels that results in individual and collaborative agency.
- Select data from a wide range of sources to focus attention on what is valued rather than what is easily measured.

West-Burnham and Ireson (2005: 18) draw on the work of Richard Boyatzis and others (see Goleman et al., 2002) to recognise that becoming an authentic leader is not an event, but a set of complex relationships and interactions. Effective leadership is rooted in personal authenticity, which itself is demonstrated in the interaction of values, behaviours, and language. Moreover, the development of such authenticity is a learning process, which requires reflection, awareness, and the practice of skills and social relationships over time. As Bennis and Goldsmith (1997: 7) put it:

> the process of becoming a leader is much the same as the process of becoming an integrated human being.

For those leading on the second horizon this also means learning to live with tensions, ambiguity, and mess. It will involve making mistakes and, much more importantly, learning from them. In a classic *Harvard Business Review* article, Peter Drucker (2008 [1999]: 3) suggested:

> Whenever you make a key decision or take a key action, write down what you expect will happen. Nine or 12 months later, compare the actual results with your expectations.

Drucker called this self-reflection process feedback analysis, saying it was the 'only way to discover your strengths' (2008 [1999]: 3).

The second horizon can therefore be an uncomfortable place from which to lead. It is best not to journey alone, but to seek fellow travellers. This is one reason why heads working with Schools of Tomorrow decided, with support from the Fore Trust,[1] to form the Schools of Tomorrow Fellowship.[2] It is open to all schools but commits those who choose to join to a long-term research and development partnership, based around mutual support and challenge, with other schools beyond their immediate context who share the same values, the same understanding of change, and the same ambition to engage their stakeholders differently as part of that journey. Through this partnership, as Julie Taylor puts it, 'We are being challenged to think in a different way.'

If you have read this far, even if you started with Part Three, we hope you have been challenged to think in a different way about leadership and school purpose, and have been encouraged to affirm, or reaffirm, your basic values as a leader and educator. Perhaps, in turn, this may have encouraged you to engage differently with all your stakeholders so as to consider together what possibilities you could open up for your school and its communities.

The diversity of schools in England, in particular, today means that the circumstances in which school leaders work do vary considerably, even between neighbouring schools in very similar contexts. Any leader must carefully choose the context in which to work, and cultivate a clear understanding and articulation of their own values to ensure a good fit with any school they may lead.

If you are taking on the leadership challenge, whatever your circumstances, we want you to know you are not alone. We urge you to grow your own authenticity, to create purposeful and supportive alliances with others, and to collect, scrutinise, and share evidence about the impact of the changes you decide to implement. Importantly, be sure to also allow yourself time to regularly sustain your own personal renewal.

---

1   See http://www.thefore.org/.
2   See http://www.schoolsoftomorrow.org/trailblazer.html.

If you are reading this as a governor or trustee, remember the example of the governors who appointed Andrew Morrish. Avoid knee-jerk, narrow, or blinkered responses. A radical approach to change, going back to the roots, requires time, commitment, and courage. Make explicit when recruiting – especially for leadership positions – the philosophy, culture, and ethos of the school to avoid later tensions and conflict.

If you are a policy-maker, on whatever scale, remember when making decisions that there are no straight lines of cause and effect, and no simple metrics by which to judge success. So, your role is to create the best possible conditions in which systemic organic growth can occur, providing light and air, nutrients and time – whilst standing back to allow it to happen, without trying to direct it minutely. Pulling up plants just to check on their root growth is generally not a good idea for the long term.

We all need to recognise that the second horizon is fundamentally about optimism. Leadership for tomorrow is grounded in a belief in the huge potential within all of us, which is far from being fully tapped in the present. The way to better fulfil that potential starts with seeing children and young people as human beings in the round, not through a partial or narrow focus, and involves recognising that they, their families, and communities share the privilege of being both learners and educators. It involves being honest about the limitations of our successes so far and thinking creatively about how to grow in different ways. It means respecting, but not being constrained by, the demands of the first horizon today, whilst keeping a clear but measured eye on the future third horizon.

In other words, it is time for the leadership of schools, individually and collectively, to become truly connected.

Questions for reflection and discussion

- Reflecting on this chapter and all that has gone before, what changes do you now feel you want to lead?
- What are the implications of this for yourself and your personal development? Consider this in terms of your own values, behaviour, and skills, and identify specific areas you want to follow up.
- Where will you look for sources of personal support in bringing about the changes you are seeking?

Futureword

The future is not preordained and handed down to us. It does not arrive out of nowhere. It is shaped and influenced by what each of us thinks and imagines, believes and feels, and says and does today, as well as by natural forces that we do not control. It is not simply a continuation of the past, although it will have roots that can be found there. It is not inevitably an improvement, but we can try hard to make sure that we make better judgements and do not repeat old mistakes.

We have argued throughout this book that change in our understanding of schooling is needed to better prepare young people to meet and shape their futures. We have sought to identify directions but not to prescribe rigid solutions. We have also posed a number of questions throughout to stimulate thinking about the issues raised and argued that responses will vary in different contexts. In nearly all cases, these questions are based in the present, raising implications for the future.

Our final change study attempts to draw together some of the hazy images from the third horizon into a possible coherent future. Based in a hypothetical future context, we imagine one possible vision of education and community by applying some of the key issues and themes found throughout the book. This outlook is deliberately optimistic, whilst recognising that significant difficulties will be encountered in the intervening years.

It is not the only possible future, nor is it necessarily the most desirable. It is most certainly not a prediction. Its purpose is simply to stimulate thinking and discussion for you and your colleagues about your own direction of travel. If it is to be judged, it should be on the basis of whether, as one possible direction of travel, it offers a richer and fuller expression of the principles and values contained in the four propositions from Chapter 1 than we have in practice today. If so, as leaders today, how can we move towards shaping such a better tomorrow?

Questions for reflection and discussion

- In what ways are the leadership challenges facing Danielle D'Air similar to, and different from, those that you and other school leaders face today? To what extent does she show characteristics of leadership for tomorrow?
- What would your own preferred future look like? What steps can you take today to move closer towards it?
- How might you use this scenario to foster debate and thinking with colleagues about your future direction of travel?

Change study 6: A day in the life – 2040

So what might tomorrow look like? Here is one view from the third horizon.

Danielle D'Air woke early at 4.30 a.m. and quietly prepared herself for her first appointment of the day – the virtual meeting of the Discovery Global Learning Community Executive Team. She quickly tidied the conservatory of her home and closed the door to the rest of the house so as not to wake the others. She had found it difficult to adjust to meeting with her colleagues as holograms initially, uncertain of how to react. Naturally a tactile person, she still remembered with vestiges of horror the first time she reached out to put her hand on Salin's arm and it went straight through him. However, since the team was spread over six continents and nine countries, it was essential that their monthly meetings were held virtually and on a rota of different times to take account of the time zones.

After 90 intense minutes, she said goodbye to her global colleagues, pleased with what had been achieved. Her proposals for hosting next year's annual international student conference were very well received, and they could progress to the next stage of planning, including managing the selection of their delegates. There would be strong competition for places, despite the lack of opportunity to visit another country.

She had also managed to trade some of her subscription for virtual teaching units to her partner learning communities in Gambia and Nepal. She found this was one of the hardest parts of the budget to manage as units had to be purchased in advance, meaning they each had to predict which personalised programmes students would opt into. Fortunately, all the learning communities faced the same problems and, more often than not, they found ways to help each other out. This year, they had all experienced an increased demand for face-to-face tutor groups, a move away from the virtual learning experiences that had been popular for the last few years.

Danielle had also been very impressed with the short presentation she'd seen of a next generation structured learning search platform and had agreed to become a pilot school in its trial. At last technology companies and educators seemed to be making progress in presenting students with choices as they searched the internet, developing their critical understanding, and making them aware of when information is considered contentious for different reasons. Finally, all her colleagues had agreed to contribute to their collective investment in further developing active learning accounts (ALAs) in order to personalise learners' records. As she quickly ate breakfast with her two oldest children, Danielle felt the day had started well.

As executive coordinator of the Ash Valley Learning Community (AVLC), in the second year of her four-year term, she still felt exhilarated each day by the range and breadth of the learning that took place in the community and extended to networks throughout the world. Her role often left her exhausted by the end of the day, and her partner frequently commented that she was either too tired to speak coherently or that she gabbled incomprehensively about all that had happened during the day. She was continually amazed at the creativity and enterprise of the community, and described her greatest challenge as ensuring that each individual and learning group was listened to and received a timely response.

The hardest lesson for AVLC had been how to recognise success whilst trying to keep track of all the groups and networks that interacted continuously, and to redefine how to support, facilitate, and record progress. The monthly meetings of the Ash Valley Council had become very important in terms of feedback, with a diverse range of information presented – never comprehensive, but always surprising as new projects came to the fore and well-established, familiar ones made sudden innovations or changes of direction. The decision some years back to encourage contributions in different media had also meant that council meetings were no longer just a talking shop but entertaining and thought-provoking. Later, Danielle would meet with members of a dance group – all disengaged teenage students – together with their support worker and the director of personalised learning, to follow up on their performance in the council meeting the previous Wednesday.

Having finished her breakfast, Danielle went to one of the small enterprise parks in Ash Valley. Today she was visiting two units on the compact site – the Ash Valley Bespoke Wood Company and the Digital Media Exchange. First, she was going to see Bismarck, a refugee from Somalia who she had been mentoring for five years, since he arrived in the UK. Her decision to continue as his mentor when she was appointed as executive coordinator had been questioned by many, but she felt a commitment to him and thought it important to show by example that the individual student always comes first.

Now 14 years old, Bismarck was showing, for the first time, a commitment to improving his literacy and numeracy skills. For the first two and a half years it was difficult to engage him in anything other than practical work and rugby, and even in those activities his frustrations could erupt into aggression and violence. The objective of the day's meeting was to persuade Bismarck to accept a major shift in his active learning programme, to intensify the academic content and minimise the practical elements. Danielle discovered that Bismarck's rugby coach had already achieved this. Bismarck, with his coach quietly watching in the background, proudly showed her his revised ALA and informed her that she did not need to waste her time with him any more.

Her visit to the Digital Media Exchange was less positive, however. Once one of the most popular and successful enterprise projects, which could not meet the demand for places, it was now struggling to attract both commissions and students who wanted to follow its training programmes. As a result, it was no longer viable and could not be allowed to continue unless fortunes changed dramatically soon. The collective behind the project had once received awards for their innovative work and, concerned about this downturn, had asked to meet with Danielle personally to discuss the future. She left after an hour, disheartened by their attitude and resistance to coming up with new ideas. She wondered how they could reinvigorate the group and the project, which she considered still had an important role to play.

AVLC had evolved gradually over a period of almost 20 years. Danielle had first come to live in the area 12 years ago and her initial involvement was as a first-time mother through her new baby. Her own excitement in learning was rekindled and she became a student of human development and then a volunteer mentor. Some people traced the origins of the learning community back to the Ash Valley MAT, a group of seven primary and two secondary schools formed initially in 2017. Others offered an alternative perspective, emphasising the role of the local council, area health authority, university, further education college, and Chamber of Commerce, amongst others. Danielle always stressed that what had been achieved so far had come from the contributions and commitments of many disparate groups and the willingness of everyone to work together, working to the principle, 'Look after each other to help yourself'.

In the early stages, there were many contentious debates to be resolved about what was in the best interests of the community as a whole. When taking up her position as executive coordinator, her predecessor had said that she would need to be vigilant in reinforcing the core principles and not become complacent, believing that everything would continue to work smoothly. She counted herself fortunate that the number of issues of this type were nothing like those faced by her predecessors (thanks to their relentless determination in laying the groundwork), but she estimated that she explicitly referred to the principles and values of the learning community at least five times each day.

AVLC notionally covers an area with an ethnically diverse population of almost 100,000 people. Economic activity is very varied. The two largest employers are in the health and learning sectors, but the roles of those working in these areas continue to evolve. Everyone Danielle knows is consistently following a learning programme of one type or another, and often whether that is for personal or professional development is indistinguishable. Most other employment is in small manufacturing units (e.g. making energy-saving doors and windows) or in the service or maintenance industries, with many self-employed.

The big change to employment and attitudes to work came when the government radically overhauled the benefits system to provide a universal wage to everyone over 18. Rather than encouraging idleness, as its detractors feared, it enabled individuals to have more choice over what they did and valued. Many people continue to earn additional income from a variety of different sources and choose when and how to work. It is common for people to differentiate between work done for money alone and work from which they gain other satisfactions.

Gradually people began to show more interest in learning and took increased responsibility for themselves and for those around them. Danielle's friends and colleagues often discuss whether the social disruption and disorder of the 2020s could have been avoided. In any case, out of the mess and chaos, the varied initiatives of communities, voluntary and religious organisations, and public services had begun to have an impact.

These community initiatives also related well to the way the MAT was changing learning in the schools at the time, and to some of the college and university's new courses and programmes. The ethnically diverse communities of the area also meant that global networks were already established and, as one academy principal used to say, 'We just had to open the doors and make the connections, instead of closing ourselves off from each other.'

Today, in 2040, there are more people enrolled in AVLC than the population of the immediate local area, as no one is turned away. But everyone is expected to maintain an ALA. Danielle was very proud of the fact that less than 5% of learning accounts remain inactive for more than a month, and over half of these belong to the elderly or long-term sick. All children are registered at birth and the percentage of centenarians enrolled is now over 2% and increasing. Lifelong learning throughout the community is becoming a reality.

The ALA had replaced the progress and achievement record (PAR) as the way in which students of all ages maintain a log of their learning and attainment. The change in name marked a shift towards students having personal responsibility for their own learning, rather than the school or college keeping records to which the students contributed. Controversial when introduced, there are now different versions of the ALA, partly determined by age, developmental progress, and, for older students, the level of commitment they wish to make. As a consequence, it is common to find mixed-age learning groups, with students engaging in different purposes but aiming for common learning objectives.

Whilst the ALA is a formal record of the student's learning, it is the process around it that is key to its importance and success. Every student has a personal tutor, with levels of support varying depending on the programme they are following. In the early years (from birth to at least 18 years of age) the tutor's involvement is most intensive, with responsibility for planning, monitoring, and amending the learning programme, providing counselling, and arranging additional interventions if required. Learning programmes include social, cultural, and sporting activities throughout the day, seven days a week. Learning is no longer confined to an institutionally set day, whilst the learner is seen as a whole person. Starting the learning programme at birth had also achieved marked improvements in average levels of attainment and attitudes to learning, as all children make progress in the essential early years of development. The early years team – which includes midwives, health visitors, and child development professionals – works with parents and young children, engaging parents and carers in learning, as well as ensuring that every child receives a range of formative experiences.

The tutors are all trained professionals. Whilst some also undertake other educational roles – such as teaching, supporting, or facilitating learning – being a tutor has high status as this is the key role for the student. The responsibility and accountability for the learning account sits with the student, but the relationship between the tutor and student is of central importance. Older students could vary their level of support, depending upon their learning programme and requirements. Tutors are very skilled and support each other to ensure that demands placed on them are reasonable and stay within defined professional boundaries.

Danielle's next meeting of the day was with the primary years learning programmes team, responsible for learners aged 4–12. At the meeting were tutors, curriculum programme managers, and representatives from the well-being support team. As Danielle walked to the learning centre where the meeting was being held, she was surprised to meet Jayla.

Jayla would be 11 years old next month and was one of the most academically gifted students ever to have studied at AVLC. There had, however, been concerns from a very early age about her social development and willingness to engage with others. Jayla and her parents had chosen an intensive learning programme that had meant she was almost exclusively isolated from other children. Her proficiency and attainment in a wide range of areas was exceptional, but concerns about her isolation and withdrawal have intensified as she has grown older.

Danielle was delighted to see Jayla and asked her what she was doing. Jayla explained briefly that her tutor and a specialist counsellor had been setting her learning objectives that involved her meeting and working with many other people. She said she was coming in today because she wanted to change her learning programme to include class-based activities and a group residential course. She then added that she also wanted to become a student representative on the curriculum planning committee as she had some ideas she wanted to present. Danielle struggled to hide her excitement, and told Jayla how good it was to see her and how pleased she was that her learning was progressing so well. She asked Jayla for permission to look at her full ALA so she could see how this progress had been recorded.

The main topic of discussion for the primary years learning programmes team was balancing the number of students who were on full-time, site-based programmes. This was a constant area for negotiation between the various professional teams. Danielle often felt her role was to act as arbiter between what could easily become conflicting interests and perspectives. There was also the practical challenge of how to manage the available resources with the personalised programmes and needs of individual students. As the discussion began to follow its normal pattern, she interrupted the flow to tell everyone about her encounter with Jayla. Danielle asked, 'What should we have done differently to support Jayla's development?' There was a long silence, before someone said, 'Nothing.' Danielle suggested that they should focus on how they could continue to improve what they were doing for the benefit of all the students, balancing the needs of developing children – and the inherent tensions they will experience – with the available resources.

Danielle had two more appointments in her diary that day, but decided to drop in to a case review meeting of the family support multi-agency team. She always found that these stimulated and challenged her thinking, as most of those attending came from health and social services backgrounds. The group worked in a very disciplined way, spending five minutes on each case, on average. Everyone was well informed about the details and offered suggestions for appropriate actions. Decisions were quickly reached and recorded, and implementation always began within two days of the meeting. Whilst family members were not invited to the meetings, they were informed that their circumstances would be discussed and that they would be told the outcome within 24 hours. Feedback from families suggested that whilst they did not like the process, they understood it was in their best interests and was not designed to be punitive. As a consequence, the effectiveness of interventions had improved considerably and families were more responsive in many ways, including in their collective engagement in learning.

Over a quick lunch, Danielle's plans to catch up on messages with her PA were interrupted by several colleagues wishing to discuss various matters. Following these discussions, she was late arriving at the opening of the Future Story exhibition. She could hear the buzz of animated conversation and laughter as she approached the building where the event was being held. Future Story had begun as a small local history project for students in their early teens; a group who were disaffected from their local community and had no clear sense of identity. Older residents had initially been involved to provide an oral history of life in the twentieth century. The groups' learning facilitators allowed the conversations between the younger and older learners to develop, and found that they began to talk about the future as well as the past. Gradually, a new programme for all ages had developed out of this – a programme that combined historical research, analysis of current events, and the identification and exploration of future trends in the locality. The programme has become so successful that demand is now greater than available provision, and as such it has spawned several self-managing groups. The importance of the work produced to the future of the locality was evidenced by the number of politicians and senior officers from central and regional government bodies who were in attendance.

Danielle smiled to herself as she witnessed three students from the programme (aged approximately 14, 55, and 85 respectively) explaining their five-year policy ideas, based on the lessons of the past, to a well-known politician and a senior civil servant. On her way out, she followed a group of teenage learners assisting their elderly colleagues back to their mobility transport.

Before the evening meeting of the Ash Valley social capital council, Danielle had planned a meal with some of the community leaders in the area. She remained very grateful for the personal support and guidance this group had been giving her since she undertook the role of executive coordinator. She had come to rely on them for their wisdom and selfless willingness to listen and advise without ever appearing to direct.

They were a small, diverse group – an imam, a football coach, a choreographer, a theatre director, the managing director of a number of companies, and a youth leader and self-defined community activist – but Danielle was very aware that without their ability to work together, and their commitment to continuing to do so, the social capital council would not have started, or continue to thrive. Its origins lay in the social unrest of the 2020s, when young people found a voice about the sense of hopelessness they felt when it came to achieving their aspirations. Many had accused youngsters of lacking ambition and being disaffected, but this group came together and agreed to listen to what the young people had to say about what they wanted.

The aim was quickly defined as rebuilding social capital for the community as a whole. Now the programme had successfully linked all the sports, arts, and cultural organisations into a coaching programme of excellence, related to the ALA. Other offerings included: residential scholarships with global partners; the citizen award scheme (which 85% of students complete to gold standard); the annual mock United Nations forum, with groups from around the UK; and a sponsored internship programme that currently offered 150 full-time places a year, some lasting for a year or more. Meetings of the social capital council were usually attended by over 50 local organisations and groups, evidence of the high importance given to the collective investment in the area and in young people in particular.

At that night's meeting, Danielle would present outline plans for the international conference which would be held next year, and invite ideas and contributions. As always, the most interesting item on the agenda would likely be the open forum when the different groups could each give a five-minute presentation. Groups always arrived early to draw lots as the hour-long forum was never sufficient to allow everyone to contribute. Contributions varied from exchanging information, sharing successes, requesting assistance, raising concerns, and presenting ideas. Every meeting seemed to result in groups working together in new and different ways.

It was just after 9.00 p.m. when Danielle returned home from what had been an exceptionally long but successful day. She wished all days could be as positive as this, but was content for now to join her partner in listening to music and let her mind wander.

Acknowledgements

This has been, first and foremost, a book about the lived experience of school leaders today. We have tried to put a framework of thinking, ideas, and evidence around what they, their colleagues, and students have shown and told us. But that theorising has been firmly and equally grounded both in values and practice. It offers not a panacea but a way forward that we believe is a genuinely hopeful one.

To each of these school leaders we express our deep gratitude for their time, commitment, openness, honesty, and inspiration. It has been a great honour for us to spend time sharing just a small part of their journey.

We have also been privileged and grateful for the practical help and support freely given by a great number of people, many, indirectly, through their membership of and contribution to Schools of Tomorrow, and others, more directly, to the research and writing through ideas, suggestions, discussion, or encouragement at various stages over the last five years. They include: Mark Bennison, Fiona Carter, Guy Claxton, Andrew Curry, Lynn Davies, Keri Facer, Charles Fadel, Richard Gerver, Janet Goodall, Maria Kaparou, Brian Lightman, Bill Lucas, Justine Mercer, Tom Middlehurst, Ralph Tabberer, Matthew Taylor, Ian Wigston, and Sue Williamson.

Whether we have been able to do justice to all that we have learned is not for us to say. We have certainly tried, but the inevitable shortcomings remain our responsibility. We hope, nevertheless, that what we have been able to capture will be of help and encouragement to school leaders, and maybe to those to whom they are accountable, in navigating their way across a singularly difficult landscape towards a broader horizon.

References

Agerholm, Harriet (2016). Brexit: Wave of hate crime and racial abuse reported following EU referendum, *The Independent* (26 June). Available at: http://www.independent.co.uk/news/uk/home-news/brexit-eu-referendum-racial-racism-abuse-hate-crime-reported-latest-leave-immigration-a7104191.html.

Ainsworth, M. S. and Bowlby, J. (1991). An Ethological Approach to Personality Development, *American Psychologist*, 46(4): 333–341.

Audit Commission (2006). *More Than the Sum*. London: Audit Commission.

Bar-On, R. (2000). Emotional and social intelligence: Insights from the emotional quotient inventory (EQ-i), in R. Bar-On and J. D. A. Parker (eds), *Handbook of Emotional Intelligence*. San Francisco, CA: Jossey-Bass, pp. 363–388.

Bar-On, R. (2006). The Bar-On Model of Emotional-Social Intelligence (ESI), *Psicothema*, 18, suppl: 13–25. Available at: http://www.eiconsortium.org/reprints/bar-on_model_of_emotional-social_intelligence.htm.

Barber, M. and Mourshed, M. (2007). *How the World's Best-Performing School Systems Come Out On Top*. London: McKinsey & Company. Available at: http://mckinseyonsociety.com/how-the-worlds-best-performing-schools-come-out-on-top/.

Bartlett, J., Birdwell, J. and Littler, M. (2011). *The Rise of Populism in Europe Can Be Traced Through Online Behavior: The New Face of Digital Populism*. London: Demos. Available at: https://www.demos.co.uk/files/Demos_OSIPOP_Book-web_03.pdf?1320601634.

Belfield, C. and Sibieta, L. (2016). *Long-Run Trends in School Spending in England*. IFS Report 115. London: Institute for Fiscal Studies. Available at: https://www.ifs.org.uk/publications/8236.

Benn, M. and Downs, J. (2015). *The Truth about Our Schools: Exposing the Myths, Exploring the Evidence*. Abingdon: Routledge.

Bennis, W. and Goldsmith, J. (1997). *Learning to Lead*. Reading, MA: Perseus.

Booth, R. and Mason, R. (2017). Conservatives buy 'dementia tax' Google ad as criticism of policy grows, *The Guardian* (22 May). Available at: https://www.theguardian.com/politics/2017/may/22/conservatives-buy-dementia-tax-google-ad-as-criticism-of-policy-grows.

Boylan, M. (2016). Deepening System Leadership: Teachers Leading from Below, *Educational Management Administration and Leadership*, 44(1): 57–72.

Brooks, L (2017). Universal basic income trials being considered in Scotland, *The Guardian* (3 January). Available at: https://www.theguardian.com/politics/2017/jan/01/universal-basic-income-trials-being-considered-in-scotland.

Bruhn, J. and Wolf, S. (1979). *The Roseto Story: An Anatomy of Health*. Oklahoma City, OK: University of Oklahoma Press.

Bryk, A. S. and Schneider, B. (2002). *Trust in Schools: A Core Resource for Improvement*. New York: Russell Sage Foundation.

Bryk, A. S., Sebring, P. B., Allensworth, E., Luppescu, S. and Easton, J. O. (2010). *Organizing Schools for Improvement*. Chicago, IL: University of Chicago Press.

Cadwalladr, C. (2017). Who's supposed to regulate elections in the 21st century? Apparently no one, *The Guardian* (11 June). Available at: https://www.theguardian.com/commentisfree/2017/jun/10/electoral-reform-needed-to-control-money-lies-online-world.

Callaghan, J. (1976). A Rational Debate Based on the Facts. Speech delivered at Ruskin College, Oxford, 18 October. Available at: http://www.educationengland.org.uk/documents/speeches/1976ruskin.html.

Carter, D. (2016). United We Stand – An Insight into Multi Academy Trusts. Speech to the ASCL conference, Birmingham, 4 March.

Claxton, G. (2002). *Building Learning Power*. Bristol: TLO Limited.

Claxton, G. and Lucas, B. (2015). *Educating Ruby: What Our Children Really Need to Learn*. Carmarthen: Crown House Publishing.

Clifton, J. and Cook, W. (2012). *A Long Division*. London: Institute for Public Policy Research.

Colman, A. (2009). *A Dictionary of Psychology* (third edition). Oxford: Oxford University Press.

Covey, S. M. R. with Merrill, R. R. (2006). *The Speed of Trust*. London: Simon & Schuster.

Cruddas, L. (2015). *Blueprint for a Self-Improving System*. Leicester: ASCL.

Cunningham, R. and Lewis, K. (2012). *NFER Teacher Voice Omnibus 2012 Survey: The Use of the Pupil Premium*. Slough: NFER.

Curry, A. and Hodgson, A. (2008). Seeing in Multiple Horizons: Connecting Futures to Strategy, *Journal of Futures Studies*, 13(1): 1–20.

Curtis, C. (2017). How Britain voted in the 2017 general election, *YouGov* (13 June). Available at: https://yougov.co.uk/news/2017/06/13/how-britain-voted-2017-general-election/.

Darwin, C. (2006 [1859]). *On the Origin of Species by Means of Natural Selection, or the Preservation of Favoured Races in the Struggle for Life*. London: Folio Society.

Davies, L. (2014). The complexity of identity, in L. Davies, A. Hobbs and B. Trilling (eds), *Identity and Learning Part One: Preparing Young People to Shape a Future We Cannot Imagine – The Third Beauchamp Paper*, pp. 5–18. Available at: http://free.yudu.com/item/details/1933967/Identity-and-Learning-Part-1---Preparing-Young-People-to-Shape-a-Future-We-cannot-Imagine.

Deming, W. E. (2000). *The New Economics for Industry, Government, Education*. Cambridge, MA: MIT Press.

Department for Education (2010). *The Importance of Teaching: The Schools White Paper 2010*. London: HMSO. Available at: https://www.gov.uk/government/publications/the-importance-of-teaching-the-schools-white-paper-2010.

Department for Education (2016). *Education Excellence Everywhere*. London: HMSO. Available at: https://www.gov.uk/government/publications/educational-excellence-everywhere.

Desforges, C. and Abouchaar, A. (2003). *The Impact of Parental Involvement, Parental Support and Family Education on Pupil Achievement and Adjustment: A Literature Review*. DfES Research Report RR433. Nottingham: Department for Education and Skills.

Doward, J. and Gibbs, A. (2017). Did Cambridge Analytica influence the Brexit vote and the US election?, *The Observer* (4 March). Available at: https://www.theguardian.com/politics/2017/mar/04/nigel-oakes-cambridge-analytica-what-role-brexit-trump.

Drath, W. H. (2003). Leading Together: Complex Challenges Require a New Approach, *Leadership in Action*, 23(1): 3–7.

Drucker, P. F. (2008 [1999]). *Managing Oneself.* Harvard Business Review Classics. Boston, MA: Harvard Business School Publishing Corporation.

Edgar, D. (2001). *The Patchwork Nation: Re-thinking Government – Re-building Community.* Sydney: HarperCollins.

Electoral Commission (2016). EU Referendum Results. Available at: https://www.electoralcommission.org.uk/find-information-by-subject/elections-and-referendums/past-elections-and-referendums/eu-referendum/electorate-and-count-information.

Elliott, L. (2016). Much like the Queen, we're all going to be working a lot longer, *The Guardian* (24 April). Available at: https://www.theguardian.com/money/2016/apr/24/longevity-queen-life-expectancy-older-people-working-retirement.

Facer, K. (2011). *Learning Futures: Education, Technology and Social Change.* Abingdon: Routledge.

Fadel, C., Bialik, M. and Trilling, B. (2015). *Four-Dimensional Education: The Competencies Learners Need to Succeed.* Boston, MA: Centre for Curriculum Redesign.

Faith Survey (2016). Christianity in the UK (15 September). Available at: https://faithsurvey.co.uk/uk-christianity.html.

Field, J. (2008). *Social Capital.* Abingdon: Routledge.

Foster, R. (2005). Leadership and Secondary School Improvement: Case Studies of Tensions and Possibilities, *International Journal of Leadership in Education: Theory and Practice*, 8(1): 35–52. DOI: 10.1080/1360312042000299233.

Fullan, M. (ed.) (2003). *The Moral Imperative of School Leadership.* London: Sage.

Fullan, M. (2007). *The New Meaning of Educational Change* (3rd edition). Abingdon: Routledge.

Gallie, W. (1955). Essentially Contested Concepts, *Proceedings of the Aristotelian Society*, 56: 167–198. Available at: http://www.jstor.org/stable/4544562.

Gardiner, L. (2016). *Stagnation Generation: The Case for Renewing the Intergenerational Contract.* London: Resolution Foundation. Available at: http://www.resolutionfoundation.org/publications/stagnation-generation-the-case-for-renewing-the-intergenerational-contract/.

Garratt, D. and Forrester, G. (2012). *Education Policy Unravelled.* London: Bloomsbury.

Gladwell, M. (2009). *Outliers: The Story of Success.* London: Penguin.

Goleman, D. (1995). *Emotional Intelligence: Why It Can Matter More Than IQ for Character, Health and Lifelong Achievement.* New York: Bantam.

Goleman, D., Boyatzis, R. E. and McKee, A. (2002). *The New Leaders: Transforming the Art of Leadership into the Science of Results.* London: Little, Brown.

Goodall, J. (2014). Re-thinking engagement, in M. Groves and A. Hobbs (eds), *Growing Engagement: Re-imagining Relationships Between Schools, Families and Communities – The Second Beauchamp Paper*, pp. 10–19. Available at: http://content.yudu.com/Library/A2p4r9/GrowingEngagementRei/resources/index.htm?referrerUrl=http%3A%2F%2Ffree.yudu.com%2Fitem%2Fdetails%2F1676471%2FGrowing-Engagement---Re-imagining-relationships-between-schools--families-and-communities.

Goodhart, C. A. E. (1975). Problems of Monetary Management: The UK Experience, in *Papers in Monetary Economics*, Volume 1. Reserve Bank of Australia.

Gorard, S. (2009). Serious Doubts about School Effectiveness, *British Educational Research Journal*, 36: 745–766.

Gordon, M. F. and Seashore Louis, K. (2009). Linking Parent and Community Involvement with Student Achievement: Comparing Principal and Teacher Perceptions of Stakeholder Influence, *American Journal of Education*, 116(1): 1–32.

Gratton, L. and Scott, A. (2016a). Our life in three stages – school, work, retirement – won't survive much longer, *The Guardian* (4 September). Available at: https://www.theguardian.com/commentisfree/2016/sep/04/reaching-100-new-norm-transform-very-shape-of-life.

Gratton, L. and Scott, A. (2016b). *The 100-Year Life: Living and Working in an Age of Longevity*. London: Bloomsbury.

Greany, T. (2015). *The Self-Improving System in England: A Review of Evidence and Thinking*. Leicester: ASCL.

Groves, M. (2013). The Contribution of Student Leadership to School Transformation, *Exchanges: The Warwick Research Journal*, 1(1): 123–141. Available at: http://exchanges.warwick.ac.uk/exchanges/index.php/exchanges/article/view/3.

Groves, M. (2014). An Investigation into the Inter-Connectedness of Trust, Community Engagement, School Leadership and Educational Outcomes in English Secondary Schools. PhD thesis, Centre for Education Studies, University of Warwick. Available at: http://wrap.warwick.ac.uk/66079/.

Groves, M. (2016). *Bedford Schools Well-being Strategy: An Evaluation*. Bedford: Peter Pan Teaching School Alliance. Available at: http://www.schoolsoftomorrow.org/uploads/publications/Peter%20Pan%2080pg_Feb17.pdf.

Gunter, H. (2016). *An Intellectual History of School Leadership Practice and Research*. London: Bloomsbury.

Gutman, L. and Vorhaus, J. (2012). *The Impact of Pupil Behaviour and Wellbeing on Educational Outcomes*. Research Report DFE-RR253. London: Department for Education. Available at: https://www.gov.uk/government/publications/the-impact-of-pupil-behaviour-and-wellbeing-on-educational-outcomes.

Hansen, M. T. (2009). When Internal Collaboration Is Bad for Your Company, *Harvard Business Review*, 87(4): 82–88.

Harari, Y. N. (2016). *Homo Deus: A Brief History of Tomorrow*. London: Harvill Secker.

Hargreaves, A. and Fullan, M. (2012). *Professional Capital*. Abingdon: Routledge.

Hargreaves, D. (2001). A Capital Theory of School Effectiveness and Improvement, *British Educational Research Journal*, 27: 487–503.

Hargreaves, D. (2011). *Leading a Self-Improving School System*. Nottingham: NCSL.

Harris, A. and Goodall, J. (2007). *Engaging Parents in Raising Achievement: Do Parents Know They Matter?* DCSF Research Report RW004. London: Department for Children, Schools and Families. Available at: http://dera.ioe.ac.uk/6639/.

Hill, A., Mellon, L., Laker, B. and Goddard, J. (2016). The One Type of Leader Who Can Turn Around a Failing School, *Harvard Business Review* (20 October). Available at: https://hbr.org/2016/10/the-one-type-of-leader-who-can-turn-around-a-failing-school.

Hobby, R., Jerome, N. and Gent, D. (2005). *Connected Leadership: A Model of Influence for Those Without Power*. London: Hay Group.

Holt-Lunstad, J., Smith, T. B. and Layton, J. B. (2010). Social Relationships and Mortality Risk: A Meta-analytic Review, *PLOS Medicine*, 7(7), e1000316. Available at: https://doi.org/10.1371/journal.pmed.1000316.

Hubbard, D. W. (2010). *How to Measure Anything: Finding the Value of Intangibles in Business*. Hoboken, NJ: John Wiley and Sons.

Huppert, F. A. (2014). The State of Wellbeing Science: Concepts, Measures, Interventions, and Policies. *Wellbeing: A Complete Reference Guide*, 6(1): 1–49.

Institute for Fiscal Studies (2015). Education Spending (29 September). Available at: https://www.ifs.org.uk/tools_and_resources/fiscal_facts/public_spending_survey/education.

Institute for Fiscal Studies (2017). New funding formula could imply further cuts to per-pupil spending of 7% for around 1,000 schools after 2019–20 [press release] (22 March). Available at: https://www.ifs.org.uk/publications/9076.

Jerrim, J. (2013). *The Reading Gap: The Socio-economic Gap in Children's Reading Skills: A Cross-National Comparison Using PISA 2009*. London: Sutton Trust.

Jerrim, J. and Shure, N. (2016). *Achievement of 15-Year-Olds in England: PISA 2015 National Report*. London: Department for Education.

Laevers, F. (2003). Experiential education: Making care and education more effective through well-being and involvement, in F. Laevers and L. Heylen (eds), *Involvement of Children and Teacher Style: Insights from an International Study on Experiential Education*. Studia Pedagogica 35. Leuven: Leuven University Press, pp. 13–24.

Lasker, R., Weiss, E. and Miller, R. (2001). Partnership Synergy: A Practical Framework for Studying and Strengthening the Collaborative Advantage, *The Millbank Quarterly*, 79(2): 179–205.

Lewis, P. (2017). The politics of personal data: Is the government protecting us or neglecting us?, *The Guardian* (11 July). Available at: https://www.theguardian.com/commentisfree/2017/jul/11/the-politics-of-personal-data-is-the-government-protecting-us-or-neglecting-us.

Maak, T. (2007). Responsible Leadership, Stakeholder Engagement, and the Emergence of Social Capital, *Journal of Business Ethics*, 74: 329–343.

MacBeath, J. (2006). *School Inspection and Self-evaluation: Working with the New Relationship*. Abingdon: Routledge.

Maher, B. (2008). Poll Results: Look Who's Doping, *Nature*, 452: 674–675. Published online 9 April. Available at: http://www.nature.com/news/2008/080409/full/452674a.html.

Mason, P. (2015). *PostCapitalism: A Guide to Our Future*. London: Penguin Random House.

Miller, P. (2010). *Smart Swarm: Using Animal Behaviour to Organise Our World*. London: HarperCollins.

Ministry of Defence (2014). *Strategic Trends Programme: Strategic Global Trends – Out to 2045*. London: Ministry of Defence.

Moore, P. (2016). How Britain Voted, *YouGov* (27 June). Available at: https://yougov.co.uk/news/2016/06/27/how-britain-voted/.

Moreno, M., Mulford, B. and Hargreaves, A. (2007). *Trusting Leadership: From Standards to Social Capital*. Nottingham: NCSL.

Morrish, A. (2016). *The Art of Standing Out: School Transformation, to Greatness and Beyond*. Woodbridge: John Catt.

Muijs, D. (2010). Effectiveness and disadvantage in education: Can a focus on effectiveness aid equity in education?, in C. Raffo, A. Dyson, H. Gunter, D. Hall, L. Jones and A. Kalambouka (eds), *Education and Poverty in Affluent Countries*. Abingdon: Routledge, pp. 85–96.

Murphy, J. (1992). *The Landscape of Leadership Preparation*. Newbury Park, CA: Corwin.

NHS Choices (2016). Causes of Obesity. Available at http://www.nhs.uk/Conditions/Obesity/Pages/Causes.aspx.

Nottingham, J. (2009). The Learning Pit, *Reflections from a World of Education* [blog] (15 June). Available at: https://sustainedsuccess.wordpress.com/2009/06/15/the-learning-pit/.

Nowak, M. A. with Highfield, R. (2012). *Supercooperators: Altruism, Evolution, and Why We Need Each Other to Succeed*. New York: Free Press.

Office for National Statistics (2014). *2011 Census Analysis – Distance Travelled to Work*. Statistical release (26 March). Available at: http://webarchive.nationalarchives.gov.uk/20160107181447/http://www.ons.gov.uk/ons/dcp171776_357812.pdf.

Office for National Statistics (2015). *Life Expectancy at Birth and Age 65 by Local Areas in England and Wales: 2012 to 2014*. Statistical bulletin (4 November). Available at: https://www.ons.gov.uk/peoplepopulationandcommunity/birthsdeathsandmarriages/lifeexpectancies/bulletins/lifeexpectancyatbirthandatage65bylocalareasinenglandandwales/2015-11-04.

Office for National Statistics (2017). *Population Estimates for UK, England and Wales, Scotland and Northern Ireland: Mid 2016*. Statistical bulletin, (22 June). Available at: https://www.ons.gov.uk/peoplepopulationandcommunity/populationandmigration/populationestimates/bulletins/annualmidyearpopulationestimates/latest.

Ofsted (2013). *School Report: Pershore High School*, 16–17 July.

Ofsted (2016). *Maintained Schools and Academies Inspection Outcomes as at 31 March 2016*. Statistical release (29 June). Available at: https://www.gov.uk/government/statistics/maintained-schools-and-academies-inspections-and-outcomes-as-at-31-march-2016.

Penuel, W. R. and Riel, M. (2007). The 'New' Science of Networks and the Challenge of School Change, *Phi Delta Kappan*, 88(8): 611–615.

Perkins, D. (2014). *Future Wise: Educating Our Children for a Changing World*. San Francisco, CA: Jossey-Bass.

Peters, T. and Waterman, R. H. (2015). *In Search of Excellence: Lessons from America's Best-Run Companies*. London: Profile Books.

Pink, D. (2009). *Drive: The Surprising Truth about What Motivates Us*. Edinburgh: Canongate Books.

Pont, B., Nusche, D. and Hopkins, D. (2009). *Improving School Leadership: Volume 2 – Case Studies on System Leadership*. Paris: OECD.

Pople L., Rees, G., Main, G. and Bradshaw, J. R. (2015). *The Good Childhood Report*. London: Children's Society. Available at: https://www.childrenssociety.org.uk/sites/default/files/TheGoodChildhoodReport2015.pdf.

Pring, R. (2013). *The Life and Death of Secondary Education for All*. Abingdon: Routledge.

Putnam, R. (2000). *Bowling Alone: The Collapse and Revival of American Community*. New York: Simon & Schuster.

Ridley, M. (2017). Get grades in shape: Children who run a mile every day 'perform better' in reading, writing and maths SATs, *The Sun* (21 January). Available at: https://www.thesun.co.uk/news/2668482/children-who-run-a-mile-every-day-perform-better-in-reading-writing-and-maths-sats/.

Robertson, D. and Breen, B. (2013). *Brick by Brick: How LEGO Rewrote the Rules of Innovation and Conquered the Global Toy Industry*. New York: Crown Business.

Sahlberg, P. (2011). *Finnish Lessons: What Can the World Learn from Educational Change in Finland?* New York: Teachers College Press.

Sahlberg, P. (2015). *Finnish Lessons 2.0: What Can the World Learn from Educational Change in Finland?* New York: Teachers College Press.

Seligman, M. E. (2011). *Flourish*. Sydney: Random House Australia.

Senge, P. M., Scharmer, C. O., Jaworski, J. and Flowers, B. S. (2005). *Presence: Exploring Profound Change in People, Organizations, and Society*. New York: Crown Business.

Sennett, R. (2013). *Together: The Rituals, Pleasures and Politics of Cooperation*. New Haven, CT: Yale University Press.

Sergiovanni, T. J. (1998). Leadership as Pedagogy, Capital Development and School Effectiveness, *International Journal of Leadership in Education*, 1(1): 37–46.

Shenker, J. (2017). Revealed: the insidious creep of pseudo-public space in London, *The Guardian* (24 July). Available at: https://www.theguardian.com/cities/2017/jul/24/revealed-pseudo-public-space-pops-london-investigation-map.

Sherrington, T. (2014). OfSTED Outstanding? Just Gimme Some Truth, *Teacherhead* [blog] (30 December). Available at: https://teacherhead.com/2014/12/30/ofsted-outstanding-just-gimme-some-truth/.

Silins, H. and Mulford, B. (2002). Leadership and school results, in K. Leithwood and P. Hallinger (eds), *Second International Handbook of Educational Leadership and Administration*. Norwell, MA: Kluwer Academic Press, pp. 561–612.

Social Mobility and Child Poverty Commission (2013). *Higher Education: The Fair Access Challenge*. London: Social Mobility and Child Poverty Commission. Available at: https://www.gov.uk/government/publications/higher-education-the-fair-access-challenge.

Social Mobility Commission (2017). *Time for Change: An Assessment of Government Policies on Social Mobility 1997–2017*. Available at: https://www.gov.uk/government/publications/social-mobility-policies-between-1997-and-2017-time-for-change.

Srnicek, N. and Williams, A. (2015). *Inventing the Future: Post-capitalism and a World Without Work*. London: Verso Books.

Stone-Johnson, C. (2013). Responsible Leadership, *Educational Administration Quarterly*, 50(4): 645–674. Available at: https://doi.org/10.1177/0013161X13510004.

Strathern, M. (1997). 'Improving Ratings': Audit in the British University System, *European Review*, 5(3): 305–321.

Strauss, D. (2002). *How to Make Collaboration Work*. San Francisco, CA: Berrett-Koehler.

Sylvester, D. W. (1974). *Robert Lowe and Education*. Cambridge: Cambridge University Press.

Taylor, M. (2013). Falling in Love with the 'C' Word, *RSA: 21st Century Enlightenment* (3 September). Available at: https://www.thersa.org/discover/publications-and-articles/matthew-taylor-blog/2013/09/falling-in-love-with-the-c-word.

Telegraph, The (2013). Mid Staffordshire Trust inquiry: how the care scandal unfolded (6 February). Available at: http://www.telegraph.co.uk/news/health/news/9851763/Mid-Staffordshire-Trust-inquiry-how-the-care-scandal-unfolded.html.

Trilling, B. and Fadel, C. (2009). *21st Century Skills: Learning for Life in Our Times*. San Francisco, CA: Jossey-Bass.

TUC (2015). 15 per cent increase in people working more than 48 hours a week risks a return to 'Burnout Britain', warns TUC [press release] (9 September). Available at: https://www.tuc.org.uk/news/15-cent-increase-people-working-more-48-hours-week-risks-return-%E2%80%98burnout-britain%E2%80%99-warns-tuc.

TUC (2017). Workers in the UK put in £33.6 billion worth of unpaid overtime a year [press release] (24 February). Available at: https://www.tuc.org.uk/news/workers-uk-put-%C2%A3336-billion-worth-unpaid-overtime-year.

UK Commission for Employment and Skills (2014). *The Labour Market Story: An Overview*. Rotherham and London: UKCES. Available at: https://www.gov.uk/government/uploads/system/uploads/attachment_data/file/343448/The_Labour_Market_Story-_An_Overview.pdf.

UNICEF (1989). *The United Nations Convention on the Rights of the Child*. Available at: https://www.unicef.org.uk/what-we-do/un-convention-child-rights/.

UNICEF (2007). *Child Poverty in Perspective: An Overview of Child Well-Being in Rich Countries*. Innocenti Report Card 7. Florence: UNICEF Innocenti Research Centre.

UNICEF Office of Research (2013). *Child Well-Being in Rich Countries: A Comparative Overview*. Innocenti Report Card 11. Florence: UNICEF Innocenti Research Centre.

United Nations, Department of Economic and Social Affairs, Population Division (2014). *World Urbanization Prospects: The 2014 Revision*. Available at: https://esa.un.org/unpd/wup/Publications/Files/WUP2014-Report.pdf.

United Nations, Department of Economic and Social Affairs, Population Division (2017). *World Population Prospects: The 2017 Revision, Key Findings and Advance Tables*. Working Paper No. ESA/P/WP/248. New York: United Nations. Available at: https://esa.un.org/unpd/wpp/Publications/Files/WPP2017_KeyFindings.pdf.

Wenger, E. (1998). *Communities of Practice: Learning, Meaning, and Identity*. Cambridge: Cambridge University Press.

West-Burnham, J. (1997). *Managing Quality in Schools: Effective Strategies for Quality-Based School Improvement*. London: Pitman.

West-Burnham, J. and Ireson, J. (2005). *Leadership Development and Personal Effectiveness*. Nottingham: NCSL.

Wheatley, M. J. (2006). *Leadership and the New Science: Discovering Order in a Chaotic World*. San Francisco, CA: Berrett-Koehler.

Wiliam, D. (2006). Assessment for learning: Why, what and how, in *Cambridge Assessment Network, Excellence in Assessment for Learning*. Cambridge: Cambridge Assessment Network, pp. 2–16.

Wilkinson, R. and Pickett, K. (2009). *The Spirit Level: Why Equality is Better for Everyone*. London: Allen Lane.

Wilshaw, M. (2016). Sir Michael Wilshaw's Speech at the FASNA Autumn Conference (2 November). Available at: https://www.gov.uk/government/speeches/sir-michael-wilshaws-speech-at-the-fasna-autumn-conference.

Wolf, S. and Bruhn, J. G. (1993). *The Power of Clan: The Influence of Human Relationships on Heart Disease*. New Brunswick, NJ: Transaction Publishers.

Yukl, G. (1999). An Evaluation of Conceptual Weaknesses in Transformational and Charismatic Leadership Theories, *Leadership Quarterly*, 10(2): 285–305.